PLAS

PITT
LATIN
AMERICAN
SERIES

Primary Medical Care in Chile

ACCESSIBILITY UNDER MILITARY RULE

Joseph L. Scarpaci

UNIVERSITY OF PITTSBURGH PRESS

Published by the University of Pittsburgh Press, Pittsburgh, Pa., 15260
Copyright © 1988, University of Pittsburgh Press
Feffer and Simons, Inc., London
Manufactured in the United States of America

Library of Congress Cataloging-in-Publication Data

Scarpaci, Joseph L.
  Primary medical care in Chile.

  (Pitt Latin American series)
  Bibliography: p. 167.
  Includes index.
  1. Medical care—Chile—Santiago—Utilization.
2. Medical care—Chile—Utilization. 3. Medical economics—Chile. I.
Title. II. Series. [DNLM: 1. Delivery of Health Care—Chile. 2. Health
Services Accessibility—Chile. 3. Primary Health Care. WA 395 S286p]
RA410.9.C5S27 1988   362.1'0983   87-16199
ISBN 0-8229-3823-5

Para Gilda de Los Angeles
Por haberlo compartido todo

Contents

Tables

Figures

Preface

This study focuses on the medical care patterns and processes in Chile in 1983. Research findings presented here represent fourteen months of fieldwork in Santiago, Chile, in 1983 and 1984, and one month in northern Chile and Santiago in 1981. As the recipient of a Fulbright award administered by the U.S. Information Agency, I was granted considerable flexibility in carrying out my work among numerous public agencies in Santiago. The word *Fulbright* carried wide and prestigious recognition, and I know that it opened more doors than if my source of funding were from another country or institution. Midlevel bureaucrats within the Chilean government knew of the fellowship and, to my good fortune, were forthright in providing information. There is an obvious contrast between my access to information and the strong and authoritarian rule that characterizes the Pinochet regime. This enigma, like so much of Chile's own history, is the product of a particularly strained period when Chile found itself increasingly isolated in the international community. My good fortune in acquiring primary, secondary, and archival materials came at the expense of many Chileans who, for political purposes, were denied the same information.

Though the work is written by an outsider to the Chilean public and private medical systems and thus may fail to provide insight into the subtleties of those systems (Sidel 1980), it benefits from primary data gathered in more than 200 interviews with medical care workers and consumers and from secondary data gathered from the financial archives of public health departments, from public hospitals and clinics, and from private medical practices. I had almost daily contact with both users and providers from various Chilean national medical systems, both as a researcher and, unexpectedly, as a patient. Financing data from as far back as 1962 are included in this study, so that the trends leading up to the medical care policies of the military regime are placed in proper perspective. Because much of the data are derived from unpublished materials, special care has been taken in documenting the sources as thoroughly as possible. In a few instances, public officials have requested anonymity for fear of persecution or reprisal. This has been granted. However, the proportion of this information is small, and key arguments in this book do not depend on these sources.

This review of the Chilean medical care system attempts to make a small contribution to medical geographic inquiry by demonstrating a number of methods that can be employed in assessing medical care delivery systems. The systematic reviews of financial, economic, cultural, organizational, and spatial access to primary medical care lend themselves to international comparison. I hope that readers with interests in human geography, medical care organization, public health, urban and regional planning, and Latin American studies will find this work to be of some value.

It was my good fortune to work with a number of scholars, providers, and users of medical care in both Chile and the United States. At The University of Florida I benefited from the field lectures and advice of my dissertation supervisor, César N. Caviedes, and the critical thinking of Stephen M. Golant, Lee A. Crandall, Charles H. Wood, Terry L. McCoy, A. Stewart Fotheringham, and Douglas D. Bradham.

Preliminary funding for fieldwork in Santiago was provided by Arturo Valenzuela of Duke University who, along with Heraldo Muñoz at the Institute of International Studies, University of Chile, and Manuel Antonio Garretón at the Latin American Faculty of the Social Sciences in Santiago, organized a stimulating series of seminars in Santiago in June and July of 1983. Dagmar Raczynksi of CIEPLAN was helpful in pointing out related literature and commenting on drafts and methods in the survey design of this research. Carmelo Mesa-Lago, then a visiting researcher at CEPAL in Santiago, shared related literature on medical care financing and social security. Economists Luis Riveros and Tarcisio Castañeda of the Department of Economics at the University of Chile and Jorge Rodriguez of ILADES shared their ideas about the operations of the Chilean medical care system. Juan Giaconi, former director the Centro Diagnoistico of the Catholic University of Chile and currently Minister of Health, provided bibliographic aid throughout the early stages of my research in 1981 and again in 1983–84. Marianela Iglesias of the Department of Planning, Ministry of Health, and Ernesto Miranda, National Health Fund, prodigiously sought out useful information and patiently clarified the subtleties of the Chilean medical care system. Jorge Jiménez de la Jara of the Colegio Médico procured several documents from the archives of that institution and commented on various stages of the research design.

My former mentor and colleague Bria Holcomb at the Department of Urban Studies and Public Health Program at Rutgers University created a wonderful work environment during the revision of this manuscript. Her good cheer and support were great assets.

A very special thanks is extended to Antonio Infante, the former director of the Villa O'Higgins public health clinic in La Florida, without whose help it would have been virtually impossible to meet the users and providers of primary care at that clinic. My gratitude to the users of Villa O'Higgins for their candor and for sharing their experiences with me cannot be adequately expressed. Any inaccuracies that follow, however, are mine alone.

Now more than ever, world opinion is bitterly divided over the virtues and evils of authoritarian, capitalist, socialist, and communist forms of governments. Social scientists around the world are monitoring changes as political pendulums swing in such diverse countries as the United States, France, the Philippines, Haiti, and other countries where the role of the state machinery is being redefined, either by the electorate or through revolution. As of this writing, the Chilean regime is being challenged by a coalition of political parties from across the ideological spectrum. Regardless of the fate of the regime, the free-market experiment that it has begun should not be forgotten, and the lessons that it can teach must be learned.

Primary Medical Care in Chile

I
Introduction

Public services indicate the state's role in social and economic development. The proportion of public and private funds in the provision of services varies widely in time and space yet invariably reflects the political tendencies of an administration and the current ideologies of the state. Cutbacks in federal social programs in the United States in the 1980s, for instance, reflect the belief that less government involvement in individuals' lives is desirable. A major catalyst to this fiscal conservatism was the so-called Jarvis Amendment, which appeared before the electorate in California in 1978. This amendment, often referred to as Proposition 13, lowered the ad valorem real property taxes from 3 to 1 percent. The state of California lost about seven billion dollars in foregone revenues but afforded taxpayers that much in savings. Proponents of the amendment, H. A. Jarvis and P. Gann, activists in taxpayers' organizations, argued that lower taxes can reduce the level of public-sector programs and services. Jarvis claimed that "the only way to cut the cost of government is not to give them money in the first place" (*Facts on File* 1978: 425). Cosponsor Gann added, "The government has tried to become uncle, mother and father and we simply cannot afford it anymore" (*Facts on File* 1978: 425).

Proposals and amendments against high taxes and perceived wanton government spending appeared on the ballots in fourteen other states that November. The tenet of this legislation, and indeed its appeal to the electorate, was that local, state, and national governments could provide a minimum level of public programs and services without compromising the welfare of the general public.

Fiscal retrenchment has also become evident among other industrial nations, albeit for different reasons. The governments of Helmut Kohl of West Germany and Margaret Thatcher of Great Britain have shared a similar restrictive government ideology. This shift toward fiscal retrenchment in Western Europe conflicts with a long-established tradition of state participation in the economy, especially in human service programs. At recent economic summit meetings, leaders of the industrial nations have subscribed to fiscal conservatism to the extent that it can curtail inflation. The performance of the U.S. economy during the first term of Ronald Reagan as well as the resounding approval given Reagan by the electorate in November 1984 suggest that governments can and should provide fewer community services if private sector and individual initiatives can deliver such services. In 1986, the U.S. Congress was embroiled in a budget battle that centered on the controversial Gramm-Rudman-Hollings legislation, which proposed to reduce almost every segment of the federal budget except defense, Social Security, and other entitlements not subject to legislative review.

To some extent, these policies of fiscal retrenchment are part of a backlash to the growing tide of liberalism of the post–World War II era. Adherents to this "less-government-is-better" notion in the United States have contended that the return on human investment projects in, say, medical care, is difficult to measure and does not yield commensurate returns. Furthermore, individuals must be responsible for their own health. Clearly, among nonindigents in the United States, individual life-styles seem to largely determine health status (Dever 1980). Indeed, increasing public funds for medical care in the form of national insurance or program coverage is not considered to be an adequate substitute for what individual initiative can provide. Thus a basic premise of fiscal retrenchment is that individual and private business initiatives can be comparable to state-financed ventures. However, the crucial differences between health care (a broad gamut of factors such as education, housing, life-style, and sanitation) and primary medical care (therapeutic or curative care provided by a nurse or physician) must be distinguished. Individual behavior (a health care component) is rarely a substitute for skilled medical care in developing countries, nor can it overcome what poverty imposes (Doyal and Pennell 1979).

The current trend against the growth of the state and increased social spending is also evident among developing nations. The 1970 Chilean presidential elections produced a socialist victor, Dr. Salvador Allende, whose Popular Unity government further nationalized the economy, an action that had been on the increase in the 1960s. The Allende government encouraged growing public-sector investment in the areas of mining, metal processing, transportation, medical care, and education, investment that the administration of Christian Democrat Eduardo Frei (1964–70) had initiated. But for reasons not to be considered by this present study, the Allende government was overthrown in September 1973 by the armed forces led by General Augusto Pinochet (Sigmund 1977). Supporters of the coup claimed that the Allende administration (1970–73) wreaked havoc on the nation. They objected to high unemployment, soaring inflation, rampant labor strikes, work stoppages, and land and business expropriations that were seen as preparation for the establishment of an authoritarian socialist state.

Since 1973, Chile has been ruled by Pinochet, whose self-appointed term in office is to expire in 1989, with an option to continue until 1996. The military government has forged strong ties with new and traditional business groups of the nation and has moved to dismantle the traditional political pressure groups such as political parties, labor unions, student movements, and the national electorate. Decision rules laid out by engineers, technocrats, and economists have replaced these traditional political players. The military government in Chile—referred to as a bureaucratic-authoritarian state because of its strong-arm tactics and reliance on technical guide-lines (O'Donnell 1978)—has sought the cooperation of the nation's business groups to run the financial and industrial sectors of the economy.

In contemporary Chile, the highest public officers are appointed by the president, the state's allegiance is to social control by means of increased participation from the private sector, and there is a strong sense among national leaders that the nation should be held accountable only to the international lending community. Since the congress was suspended in 1973, there have been few institutional checks and balances. More importantly, the Chilean junta has deepened its nation's dependence on international capital by increasing the foreign debt. At the same time, however, the fervent anticommunist stance of the Pinochet regime won it tacit approval from the first-term administration of Ronald Reagan, despite the civil and human rights violations committed by the regime.[1] Although the military's strong-arm tactics have been denounced by the international community, the Pinochet government has been forthright in meeting its foreign debt with international bankers.

Two aspects of Chilean history make the study of public service provision in that country of particular interest. First, in view of the age of its written constitution, Chile was until 1973 the third-oldest democratic government in modern history, following only France and the United States. While its postindependence political history has been sporadically marred by short periods of military rule, the demands of the electorate and the action of its representatives have helped to shape the "welfare state" that characterized that country prior to 1973. Second, and germane to this present research, is the fact that the Chilean medical care system has been world reknowned for its comprehensive coverage. Its medical care planning strategies have been used as models by many nations (Roemer 1985). This system, however, has changed in light of the guiding ideology of the current regime. Thus the contrast between the conservative ideology that heralds reduced social spending and a public medical system that has expanded throughout this century makes the study of contemporary Chile an inviting intellectual challenge.

Scope and Purpose of Study

This research evaluates the accessibility of primary medical care in Chile. Primary care is defined as the first level of curative or therapeutic care provided by a physician or registered nurse, who attempts to diagnose a medical episode. Accessibility is the potential to procure care; when care is realized, it becomes utilization. Primary medical care accessibility is reviewed here in its broadest conception; that is, in terms of barriers: structural, economic, demographic and organizational, and spatial. These components of accessibility are examined in chapters 2 through 5, respectively. Although each chapter builds on earlier ones in its examination of medical care accessibility, chapter 2, based on a work from *Social Science and Medicine*, provides sufficient background information to enable the other chapters then to be read separately. A review of the literature pertinent to each topic is included in each chapter.

The methodological approach is appropriately varied, reflecting the diverse nature of the research questions. Methods of analysis range from statistical techniques and computerized mapping to participant observation and interviews. This research derives from a branch of medical geography that is best represented by Joseph and Phillips's (1984) and Shannon and Dever's (1974) organizational emphasis on the delivery of medical care (see chapter 5 for a full description). They point to the importance of considering the organizational and economic structure of a given delivery system before investigating the spatial organization of a place's service network. From this perspective, medical care policy is viewed as a subset of the larger national economic and political fabric. Thus the study of the geographic accessibility of primary care facilities—a spatial relationship—is a moot endeavor if economic access cannot be gained (Rosenberg 1983a). Hence it is first necessary to understand the restructured financial system and the economic access to medical care (chapters 2 and 3). The analysis then shifts to the capital city of Santiago for the purpose of offering a "snapshot" of the primary care system of that city in 1983 (chapters 4 and 5). Chapter 5 analyzes the spatial organization of primary care in Santiago, building on a shorter piece that appeared in *Informaciones Geográficas* (Scarpaci 1984a).

This study focuses on Santiago for several reasons. Like all South American capitals except those of Brazil and Colombia, Santiago is also Chile's primate city. Human services tend to concentrate in primate cities, and nowhere in the Third World is this a greater problem than in Latin America, the most rapidly urbanizing world region. The problems of urban growth and the taxing of human service delivery systems are particularly acute in primate cities, which tend to siphon a disproportionate amount of capital resources. In Chile, however, Santiago has remained the demographic and political center since the colonial period. While interurban comparisons of primary care accessibility would provide great insights into the pressing matter of meeting basic needs throughout the nation, such an endeavor lies beyond the scope of this study.

Primary care is in many ways the most important component of a medical care system, marking the point of entry into the system. The ease of access at the primary level dictates the comprehensiveness and quality of care at subsequent levels and the extent of a population likely to receive attention. The selection of primary care as the organizational level of analysis causes some difficulties. Economic indicators of medical care are often aggregated, and it is not easy to extract the one component that relates to primary care. Moreover, the dominant consumer of medical care funds in modern Western-based systems is the hospital. When data are disaggregated, some allowance can be made for hospital activities, but this is not always the case for primary care. Every attempt has been made in this study to distinguish national-level medical care data from exclusively primary care data.

This work attempts to go beyond a mere description of a particular medical care system. Many works on international medical care systems tend to focus on the idiographic aspects of a system, thereby failing to place the operations of these systems in any number of conceptual frameworks provided by the social, public health, and health services research sciences. Others remain within strong disciplinary confines; although they provide fruitful analyses, they are limited to followers and practitioners of that particular branch of science, or to adherents to a certain ideology. Accordingly, this research has attempted to provide insight into the operations of the Chilean medical care system for a wider audience. Findings are compared with other nations in an attempt to place the changes in the Chilean medical system within an international context. The practical utility of the work is that it provides an assessment of a public delivery system that has been the object of much attention in recent years. Developing nations around the world face a number of problems exemplified by the Chilean case, such as the pressure of mounting foreign debt, the priority of military over social spending, urban growth, and the maldistribution of medical resources.

Conceptual and Empirical Components of Accessibility

One approach to medical care accessibility is to describe the attributes of the population-at-risk and the characteristics of the delivery system. A delivery system refers to the distribution and availability of medical care providers and facilities. Important aspects of the population serviced by this system are income level, age, health status, and insurance coverage. Factors that intervene between the capacity to produce services and the actual consumption of services are also included in studies of accessibility (Donabedian 1973: 419; Aday et al. 1980: 25–27).

Studies of access to medical services often produce different conclusions, depending upon which dimension of care is studied. A general framework for identifying the dimensions of care comprises structure, process, and outcome. *Structure* encompasses those institutional and enabling aspects of the distribution and availability of resources. *Process* identifies the characteristics of the population at risk and the methods of delivery, including provider-patient interactions. *Outcome* refers to the health status of the population as a result of a medical care episode and the treatment received in the medical care system. Aday et al. have elaborated a number of models in the study of medical care accessibility. They define the interaction of structure, process, and outcome as they affect access to health care "as those dimensions which describe the potential and actual entry of a given population to its health care delivery system" (1980: 26).

Accessibility can be further defined as potential versus realized medical care. Potential access emphasizes those arrangements for the rendering of care to customers, in terms of wants, needs, and resources that consumers buy in the help-seeking process. Realized access can be separated into more objective indicators of utilization as well as into subjective appraisals of the care received. These objective indicators describe the purpose, type, setting, and time span involved in the consumption of medical services. Subjective aspects of realized care draw on consumer satisfaction: patients' evaluations of the quality of care delivered, the information given to them by providers, the ease of care, and attributes of the providers themselves (Aday et al. 1980: 33–34; Donabedian 1980).

In his seminal review of medical services research, Donabedian (1973) divided medical care accessibility into two major components: socioorganizational and geographical. The former emphasizes nonspatial resources in the potential utilization of care. Morrill et al. (1970) in their Chicago study showed that physicians' referral patterns were a complex function of the hospitals where they held privileges: half of the physicians practiced at hospitals that were not the closest to their offices, and 58 percent sent patients to only one hospital. These unexpected patterns reflect the spatial organization of the city, the type of hospital (teaching, public, or proprietary), and the ethnic and racial makeup of the consumers. Thus socioorganizational factors account for accessibility in these instances.

Geographic accessibility emphasizes the "friction of space" and the constraints that travel places on getting care (Joseph and Phillips 1984; Hawley 1950: 237). Potential barriers to care can be measured in a number of ways, each suitable to a particular purpose. These measures of geographic accessibility are (1) linear distance, (2) travel distance, (3) travel time, (4) total elapsed time, and (5) travel cost. Many of these spatial dimensions are explored in chapters 4 and 5.

Various components of accessibility to medical care are illustrated in this present research. As this review of accessibility shows, its conceptualization and measurement comprise a large set of factors that influence the users. No guiding model of accessibility can be assigned in all research exercises. There is a degree of arbitrariness in socioorganizational and geographic assessments of accessibility (Donabedian 1973: 419–508). The study of the Chilean medical care system that follows presents one approach to the study of medical care accessibility.

II
The Restructuring of Medical Care Financing in Chile

As the prolonged world recession continues, its adverse economic effects compound existing problems in Third World countries. This trend suggests that defining the role of the state in financing medical care becomes an ever more complex issue, subject to a wide spectrum of opinions (Deohadar 1982; Elling 1981; Zschock 1980; Basch 1978; Benyoussef 1977; Roemer 1977a; Maxwell 1974). On one level, this issue can be viewed in terms of governments striking the critical balance between their intentions to foster fiscal austerity and their commitment to support basic social programs. Various constraints exist, however, that impede an accurate measuring of the returns on human capital investment in health and medical care (Hakim and Solimano 1978; Berg 1973). These constraints include, for example, escalating capital costs; the complex methodology used to determine measures of health status outcomes (Zweifel 1982; Donabedian 1980); and, inevitably, competition from other sectors of the national economy for the limited resources available (PAHO 1965).

This chapter focuses on the financing and delivery of medical care in order to establish a basis of reference against which other aspects of medical care accessibility can be gauged. Chile, with its population of 11.4 million in 1982, possesses one of the highest standards of living among Third World countries; it has been described as a modern welfare state (Morris 1981; James 1969). The 1973 military intervention brought to power its current ruler, General Augusto Pinochet, who has

12

vigorously pursued and subsequently attempted to institutionalize dramatic shifts in ideological and pragmatic approaches to government. The neoclassical economic practices adopted by Pinochet contrast sharply with the mixed and socialized economies of previous administrations (Malloy and Borzutsky 1982; Vergara 1981).

A brief review of the Pinochet administration's ideology and policy strategies since seizing power provides baseline insights into the discussion of state-financed versus private medical care services in Chile during this period. In its first three years, the Pinochet government imposed measures to severely cut government spending in efforts to control, and eventually reduce, the spiraling inflation plaguing the Chilean economy. The annual consumer price index (IPC, or *indice de precios al consumidor*) fell from 605 percent in 1973 to 198 percent in 1976 (Cortázar and Marshall 1980). In pursuing a neoclassical model, the government introduced austerity measures as part of a program called Operation Shock (so dubbed because of its immediate effects), and returned state-owned enterprises to the private sector. Of the 460 enterprises owned by the state in 1973, only 23 of them still remained under state control by 1980. Other actions endorsed by the neoclassical model of development were (1) the reduction of import tariffs from as high as 300 percent in 1974 to a flat 10 percent rate (except for automobiles), and (2) the unrestricted flow of foreign capital into Chile (Ffrench-Davis 1982).

This "shock treatment" was not limited to the transfer of state-owned corporations to the private sector, however. Austerity programs reduced employment in the public sector by 25 percent between 1973 and 1979. These draconian measures were formidable given the historical importance that the public sector has had in employing the broadening middle classes of Chile and the tenacity with which those employees have held onto their jobs (Martínez and Tironi 1981). Social security (mainly retirement and disability benefits) and medical care expenditures were also reduced so that the cost of Chilean labor, relatively expensive compared to other Third World nations, could better compete in the international market (Kornevall 1977). There was even some discussion about selling public hospitals to private owners, but thus far only one hospital district in central Santiago has been transferred to private management, while still being financed by public funds.

The Pinochet government was in a position to restructure and "modernize" medical care delivery after it reduced state expenditures and liberalized its economy so that private investment could be encouraged. In 1977, four out of every five medical consultations were state financed (table 1). The government sought to reduce this dependence on state support. A robust performance in other sectors of the economy led the government economic team, strong adherents of the neoclassical ideas of Nobel laureate Milton Friedman (1962), to apply free-market principles to medical care financing, thereby increasing both private-sector participation and out-of-pocket payments by consumers. The main public-sector medical system, the National Health Service, reduced its relative contri-

TABLE 1
Public and Private Medical Consultations, 1977 and 1983

Source of Care	Percentage	
	1977	1983
Public	81.4	74.7
SNSS	57.7	49.7
Other public agencies	11.5	9.7
SERMENA	12.2	15.3
Private	18.6	23.5
No care received	0.0	1.8
Total	99.9	99.0

Sources: 1977 data from Ministerio de Salud 1983, table 78, p. 50; 1983 data from Medina n.d., table 1, p. 5.

bution of medical care from 58 percent in 1978 to 50 percent in 1983. The abrupt shift in ideology in Chile reflected a widespread mood of fiscal conservatism among the industrialized nations (Fainstein and Fainstein 1982). Before joining the Reagan administration, budget analyst David Stockman and his colleague P. W. Gramm argued that sustained government medical care financing tended to "pump up" demand (Stockman and Gramm 1980). Similar views about supply-side economics in the Chilean health care sector were spelled out in two major policy statements by the Ministry of Health (Ministerio de Salud 1977; Spoerer 1973).

The impact of these recent developments in medical care policy in Chile and the changing roles of both the private and public sector in the provision of medical care are addressed in this chapter. A review of public and private perspectives on the financing and provision of social services is undertaken followed by an overview of the evolution of Chilean medical care policy in the twentieth century. The main sections of the chapter deal with the major alterations introduced in the financing and delivery of medical services in Chile. The Chilean experience illustrates problems that may be encountered when major policy changes are enacted for the benefit of short-term economic performance in the national economy.

Public and Private Perspectives on Medical Care Financing

The role the state plays in medical care delivery has been discussed in numerous works and from various perspectives (Roemer 1977b; Navarro 1974b; Sigerist 1947). Public and private medical care systems demonstrate certain characteristics that should be reviewed briefly so that the Chilean case might be placed in proper context.

On the one hand, public ownership and administration of facilities allow planners, on a limited basis at least, to arrange service delivery (Denver 1980). In particular, medical care planning guides the medical marketplace in mixed economies with either a small private sector or with an aim of cost-containment. The Canadian experience, for example, shows that medical care planning can make reasonably accurate forecasts of medical demand (Foltz et al. 1977; Roos et al. 1976; Spaulding and Spitzer 1972). The state is often the main financier of medical care when the purchasing power of the citizenry is low or, as in Canada, when the electorate determines that differential financial access to medical care is unacceptable (Blishen 1969). Thus, in a sense, state control can reduce the highly skewed distribution of medical personnel and services that inevitably occurs when consumer purchasing power is the only determinant of entry into the medical system.

On the other hand, because of the lack of competition in public medical care systems, the state influences prices and wages in the medical market. For this reason, there are fewer incentives for reducing costs in these systems than in competitive, multisystem settings (Katz et al. 1982). Furthermore, the absence of competition weakens managerial behavior. After all, public managers have little, if any, incentive to control costs if the financial rewards do not accrue directly to them (Pommerehne and Frey 1977). In addition, consumers in a state-controlled monopoly can hardly "exit" from that system (Lineberry 1977; Hirschman 1970) to express demand for changes in services. Nevertheless, a true competitive marketplace is difficult to find in any country. Government intervention in medical care, misinformation on the part of the consumer, and the existence of oligopolies weaken the neoclassical argument that true competition can be attained in the medical marketplace (Reilly and Fuhr 1983).

To be sure, consumers in the medical marketplace face special problems. They are more passive than in other markets due to their limited understanding of medical matters. The consumer and supplier are not at arm's length, as in many other markets. Rather, patients place considerable trust in their providers and relinquish power to their agents—physicians and allied health care personnel—not only because they are unfamiliar with clinical aspects of the medical system but because they know little about costs (Reilly and Fuhr 1983). Yet it is rare, even in the socialized medical systems of Eastern Europe, for consumers not to incur some financial costs, albeit nominal or token (Kaser 1976).

On the supply side of state-controlled medical systems, salaried practitioners, like management personnel, may be less cost conscious than personnel who work on a fee-for-service basis. Practitioners in state employment supposedly behave more altruistically than their counterparts in the private sector.[1] Although the state frequently becomes the principal guarantor of access to medical care, thoughtful discussion about which medical system creates the most competition will likely continue for some time. When the state provides a service, the Pareto notion of optimality (claiming that net gains in human welfare are attained only when everyone is better off or no one is worse off), although an admirable goal (Ostrom 1977), is difficult to reach when governments change hands or succumb to political pressure.

In Latin America, political favoritism has produced duplicative medical care and social security programs that accentuate social class differences (Foxley 1979; Mesa-Lago 1978). These programs, moreover, are geared to satisfy certain groups, such as unions, state employees, or the armed forces. Industrialized countries with many political parties are equally susceptible to political favoritism. In their analysis of the Italian case, for example, Fausto and Leccisotti observe that "government intervention in the health sector is not valued by its output, but according to the inputs employed thus leaving ample room for the politicians' 'discretion' in determining what to produce and how" (1981: 39).

Private ownership and financing of medical care in its purest form is rare even in the United States, the largest for-profit medical market in the world. Government intervention there includes certificate-of-need reviews, Medicare and Medicaid subsidies, and barriers to entry such as licensing and drug regulation. That nearly 40 percent of the revenues in the U.S. health care system are derived from public subsidy suggests that it is not a pure laissez-faire system (Gibson 1980).

A number of characteristics typify the mixed medical marketplace that tends to fall under the "private medical system" rubric. First, certain types of private and for-profit medical systems such as health maintenance organizations (HMOs) induce competition, which in turn can reduce medical costs. These cost savings provide greater accessibility and an improved health status for users of these systems than for those outside of them (Homer 1982; Enthoven 1981). However, medical practitioners often invest in capital equipment that raises operational costs; these costs may prevent any savings derived from competition from being passed on to the consumer.

Second, the private medical market model does not discriminate with regard to age, sex, or race: only purchasing power, as measured by direct out-of-pocket payments or commercial insurance carriers, determines access to medical care (Aday and Andersen 1975). In the United States, for instance, the "medical market" generally refers to the private health insurance market (Reilly and Fuhr 1983).

Third, private market managers and entrepreneurs are freer to adjust prices and to hire and fire employees than their counterparts in the public sector. Fourth, although the private sector may face higher start-up costs than public operations face (Furst 1981), they allocate funds with fewer restrictions than the public sector. It is precisely such versatility that sets private medical operations apart from the public system.

As Pommerehne and Frey have aptly noted, "Theoretical reasoning alone cannot settle the dispute of whether public or private production is more efficient" (1977: 227). The strengths and weaknesses of each system acquire much more meaning when applied to a specific geographic and political setting, which the following sections address.

Public Medical Policy in Chile: 1918–79

The European programs that increasingly favored public financing of medical care and social security clearly influenced Chile and other Southern Cone nations.[2] The program organization and philosophy set forth in Germany under Chancellor Bismarck in the 1880s were precedents (Arroba 1979; Roemer 1964). What has been described by Sigerist (1947) as Bismarck's attempt to undermine the encroachment of socialism in Europe developed into a labyrinth of state social programs in Europe and the Southern Cone. Throughout the present century, the public sector in Chile has provided the greatest impetus in the financing and delivery of medical care. In fact, the Chilean government is one of the oldest public financiers of medical care in the Western Hemisphere, dating back to a social security and pension program for public railroad workers in 1918. As in the industrial countries of Western Europe, the strongest trade unions in Chile also pressed for medical insurance programs for union members and their dependents. By 1925, the Chilean government had developed milk distribution programs for children and infants, disability compensation, and old-age pensions (Romero 1977).

In Chile, ideas about social equality led to the passage of two major medical insurance laws in 1938, the Workers Insurance Law and the Preventive Medicine Law (Law Decree 6174). These two laws provided medical and retirement benefits to both public and private workers. Also created in that same year was what was to become the nation's largest nonindigent medical program, the SERMENA (National Employees Medical Service; Romero 1977).

Government participation in medical care financing and delivery in Chile had steadily progressed during the 1940s so as to have warranted the creation of a central coordinating agency in 1952, the National Health Service (SNS). The pertinent legislation, Law Decree 10,383, was passed in an election year, responding to perceived voters' demands. This is a point that many cite as a justification for the presence of an authoritarian government today. Unlike civilian governments, authoritarian governments are able to articulate medical care policy without bending to political action groups that require special concessions (Hakim and Solimano 1978; Caviedes 1984, 1979; Hall and Diaz 1971). The SNS was to coordinate more than fifty health and medical programs that operated without central administration and service coordination. Most welfare boards and private charity organizations *(juntas de beneficencia)* supported by the Catholic church also fell under state administration (Goić 1979a, 1979b). However, many public and private workers who belonged to pension and medical groups called *cajas* continued with their plans, and many of them still operate today. In keeping with a well-defined trend among industrialized countries throughout the century, the Chilean medical care system evolved into an elaborate organization and bureaucracy in order to control cost while also decentralizing service delivery (Mesa-Lago 1978). Highly structured bureaucracies are not unique to industrial nations, however (Anderson 1972). Ugalde (1978) traced the development of medical care delivery in two authoritarian nations (Iran and Colombia) and concluded that program fragmentation in those settings led to poor service delivery.

State financing of medical care in Chile reached its zenith during the years of the Allende government (1970–73) but changed markedly with the introduction of incentives for the privatization of some state functions under the Pinochet regime. In response to the bureaucratic maze created by more than fifty-five social welfare programs, thirty-one programs for the elderly, and thirty-five separate curative care systems, the Chilean government once again reorganized medical services in the late 1970s. The SNS was rearranged into the National Health Service System (SNSS) in 1979, and the SERMENA was reorganized under a new entity, the National Health Fund (FONASA), under the mandate of Law Decree 2763 (figure 1). The main feature of this rearrangement was that instead of

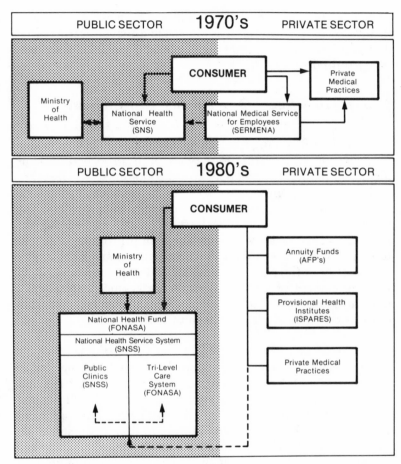

FIGURE 1. Structure of Chilean Medical Care System, 1970s and 1980s
Source: Modified greatly from Haignere 1982, figures 3 and 4.

allocating budgets to health districts, SNSS budgets were to be partially determined on a capitation basis paid to health service districts (twenty-seven nationwide). Capitation charges are now monitored by a new fee called the FAP (*factura de atención prestada)* and help to allocate budgets according to utilization of medical services instead of direct allocations that do not adjust for consumption of medical goods and services (Ministerio de Salud 1982).

Changes in Medical Care Financing in Chile in the 1980s

Medical care financing in Chile in the 1980s differs according to socioeconomic status; four types of arrangements can be identified (table 2). The upper socioeconomic strata seek private care exclusively from solo or group practices. Both ambulatory and hospital care are delivered by private providers. The upper segments of the middle classes seek care from HMO-like ISAPREs (provisional health institutes) or private medical centers. The remaining middle income groups are treated predominantly by the National Health Fund (FONASA) and pay at least 50 percent of the cost of ambulatory and hospital care. Indigent and low-income workers *(obreros)* receive care from the National Health Service System without charge.

TRANSFER OF CLINICS FROM NATIONAL TO COUNTY LEVEL

Several aspects of state-financed medical care have changed in the 1980s. One change, stipulated by Law Decree 3060, has been the transfer of a small number of public health clinics and rural health stations *(postas rurales)* from SNSS management to county-level *(municipio)* administration (Ministerio de Salud 1982). This administrative transfer (municipalization) purports to give municipal authorities more autonomy in clinic management. An innovative idea, this transfer is thought to be more cost effective because clinics are reimbursed on a capitation basis that pays slightly more than reimbursements in SNSS clinics. Municipalities administer clinics for five years, after which time contracts can be renewed. To ensure quality care, only medium-sized facilities with service populations of 40 thousand or less can participate, so that urban

service districts are more manageable in the new program (Giaconi 1982).
Government authorities base the municipalization program

TABLE 2
Medical Care Financing, by Income Group, ca. 1982

Income Group[a]	% of Total Workers	Annual Income ($)[b]	% of Total Income[b]	Occupation[c]	Source of Care[a]	Out-of Pocket Payments[a]
Low	40	962	11.5	Unskilled laborers, domestic workers, indigents, small farmers	SNSS	none
Middle	40	2,507	29.9	Retail workers, self-employed, low-level government workers, skilled laborers	FONASA; private and public pensions	Graduated scale; about half
Upper Middle	10	5,480	16.3	Professionals, high-level government workers, midlevel management	Private medical centers; ISAPREs; private providers	Graduated scale; at least 50–70%
Upper	10	14,230	42.4	Professionals, high-level technical workers, entrepreneurs	Private solo or group providers	Nearly 100%

a. Determined by author.
b. Calculated at thirty-nine pesos to the dollar. See Riveros 1983.
c. See Martinez and Tironi 1982:22.

on two notions: administrative decentralization and efficiency. The former recognizes that local government is an intermediate organization that is effective in problem solving because municipal officials "know the demands and preferences of the people" (Ministerio de Salud 1982: 3). The municipalization programs that began in 1981 and 1982 were guaranteed a minimum reimbursement for each medical consultation provided. Again, this scheme was devised to ensure fiscal support only for medical care delivered and thereby avoided the complicated procedure of projecting needs based on historical utilization data. With all curative care guaranteed by the state, however, some clinic directors broadened the scope of primary curative care to boost revenues. In some cases it was reported that clinic personnel visited elementary schools and gave vaccinations or checked oral hygiene. Curative care charges were then applied en masse. Other cases showed that clinics remained open in the evenings to tap the working-adult market. Community residents in small towns could visit the clinic in the evening and receive blood-pressure checks. This two-minute procedure received the same capitated reimbursement from the state as a twenty-minute medical consultation.

In light of these abuses and the difficulties in distinguishing between curative and preventive care, the Ministry of Health placed ceilings on the number of treatments that qualified for reimbursement. Before the end of the first year of operation, reforms were enacted to curtail runaway costs (personal communication, Servicio Metropolitano Salud Norte, 21 June, 1984). Subsequently, a number of directors of municipalized clinics expressed much unwillingness to renew contracts with national authorities (personal communications, directors of municipalized primary care facilities, April–July 1984). The fixed reimbursement ceilings limited profit making, which in turn reduced capital investment and staff increases.

Municipal authorities have expressed interest in assuming clinic management only in the best-organized and best-staffed clinics. The health district in southeastern metropolitan Santiago (comprised of low-income neighborhoods and discussed in chapter 4), for example, has had no offers, nor are such offers forthcoming (personal communication, Servicio Salud Suroriente, July 1984). High-income districts in the northeastern municipality of Las Condes, however, have had greater success in this venture.

There is no evidence that municipalization will change the efficiency of clinic operations. A more credible justification is that private management will take control in the long run, an idea alluded to in a policy statement issued by the Ministry of Health two months after the 1973 military intervention (Spoerer 1973). Thus, given the capital-generating potential of these clinics, the long-range program goal is not merely to shift management of medical facilities to another layer of public bureaucracy but to set the stage so that eventually private medical firms can manage them (Jiménez de la Jara 1982a).

NEW FEE SCHEDULES AND MEDICAL CARE FINANCING

The difficulties in establishing out-patient charges in Third World countries have been summed up well by Boland and Young (1983), who state that real costs cannot be identified; only "corresponding costs" can be derived for the purpose of estimating medical charges.

A formidable change in Chile's medical care financing resulted with the transition from the SERMENA to the FONASA. In April 1983 new price schedules for ambulatory and hospital care were instituted. Like the SERMENA, the FONASA delivers curative care to middle-income groups *(empleados)* but allows consumers to select from a greater number of providers from the public and private sectors. The SERMENA was susceptible to a number of abuses that were corrected under the FONASA. Physicians could, for example, overcharge patients (at no expense to themselves or patients) by simply filling out a voucher and later redeeming it, an abuse that has been recognized even by the Chilean Medical Society (Colegio Médico; *La*

Tercera 27 March 1983). Also, under the SERMENA patients did not have to present identification to a third party before receiving a voucher. Thus it was easy for nonmembers to gain illegal access into the SERMENA medical system even though vouchers were purchased (Ochoa 1978). To avoid these abuses, FONASA patients now present identification to third parties (bank tellers or FONASA clerks) and pay for a part of the voucher before service is rendered.

The FONASA is divided into three levels of care into which both consumers and providers (physicians, midwives, physical therapists, nurses, medical technologists, and laboratories) freely enroll. There should be no clinical difference in medical care among these levels, but younger physicians, general practitioners, and nonspecialists are concentrated in level one, while experienced specialists are concentrated in level three. This system, with its option to select a specific provider and level of care, is seen as the main attribute of the "free choice system" *(sistema de libre elección)*. At each level of care the government contributes 250 pesos (about $3) per voucher. For example, in 1983 a level-one voucher cost the patient 250 pesos, level two cost 500 pesos ($6), and level three cost 750 pesos ($9). Patients purchase a combination of vouchers (depending on the service) and turn them over to the medical practitioner upon delivery of service. In other words, the fee schedules translate into state subsidies of 50, 33, and 25 percent for the three respective levels of curative care. The government contends that "this differentiation of levels allows users to select the health care professional according to their budget and preferences" (ODEPLAN 1983, p. 79; my translation).

Publicly financed medical care in other countries is funded by a variety of schemes. Medical care programs in Japan, Norway, and the Federal Republic of Germany are operated with employer and employee contributions to insurance premiums; medical care is provided by either state employees or providers under contract to the state. In other countries, medical programs are financed by general tax revenues; in these operations, no payments for care are rendered directly by the patient, either at the time of delivery or on a monthly basis. Great Britain, China, and the USSR best exemplify this structure. Other countries blend these two types of financing. In Canada, for example, the source of funding is derived from provincial premiums as well as provincial and national treasuries (Roemer 1985). Brazil uses tariffs on agricultural exports to finance rural health services (Mach 1978).

All working Chileans other than laborers must remit a percentage of their wages to FONASA or other government-approved health systems by means of payroll deduction *(cotización)* and pay, in addition, specific curative and therapeutic charges. Mandatory payroll deduction rates rose from 4 percent in 1981 to 5 percent in January 1983 to 6 percent most recently. There is good reason to suspect that the increase is an austerity measure to confront the fiscal crisis and to meet the foreign debt payments: Chile has the second highest per capita debt in Latin America, following oil-rich Venezuela.[3] Although evidence on curative medical care financing around the world indicates that partial payment enhances the credibility of public medical services among users (Kohn and White 1976; Akin et al. 1986), the FONASA price hikes are not token costs for consumers. Real wages in Chile fell by 15 percent from 1973 to 1982 (Cortázar 1983). Furthermore, the severity of the price hikes was measured by the National Statistics Institute at 134.8 percent in the last quarter of 1983, the second highest increase among the 347 items that comprise the consumer price index (IPC; *El Mercurio* 1983a).

Beyond the normative scheme of the FONASA program is a very different record of satisfying consumer needs. A 1983 survey of 2,820 persons in Greater Santiago, undertaken by researchers from the University of Chile's School of Public Health and Gallup Chile, Inc., ranked four types of private medical systems (private clinics, prepaid group practices, private individual practices, and care given by friend or family) and four types of public medical systems (armed forces' programs, the SNSS, the FONASA, and other public programs; Medina n.d.). This ranking was based on the utilization of five kinds of medical care; that for acute conditions, chronic conditions, hospitalization, checkups, and dental problems. Users of the FONSA had the lowest average utilization rates among the eight systems for the five types of care. Furthermore, it was found that FONASA users had the highest rate (39 percent) of nonutilization for acute care needs (Medina n.d.). These findings suggest that, as a middle-income group, FONASA patients incur the greatest relative costs among all medical consumer groups, thereby reducing medical demand to the lowest levels in the nation.

A major premise of the FONASA program is that the technical competence of curative care is identical in all three of its levels: only the amenities such as office or clinic settings, waiting time, and physician specialty should vary. To date, however, no study has investigated the waiting time among FONASA patients nor their satisfaction with the new system.[4]

Supply and demand forces in the new FONASA hierarchy, as measured by the proportion of physicians and patients in each level of care, have yet to reach a state of equilibrium. Table 3 shows that patients in level one (the least expensive level of care) have the least access to physicians, while level three patients enjoy the most favorable physician-to-population

TABLE 3
Physicians and Patients in Each Level of the FONASA, 1983

Level of Care	Physicians		Patients Attended		Ratio of Physicians to Patients
	Number	%	Number	%	
One	2,839	36.3	1,552,055	48.6	1:547
Two	3,440	44.0	1,324,145	41.5	1:385
Three	1,543	19.8	319,948	10.1	1:207

Sources: Physician data, FONASA 1983a; patient data, FONASA n.d.

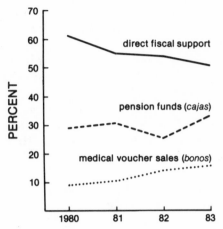

FIGURE 2. *Sources of the FONASA Operating budget,*
1980–83
Source: Compiled from FONASA 1962–83.

ratio. Physicians are clearly more attracted to the higher levels
of care, while most patients opt for the least expensive care.

A breakdown of income sources during the first three years
of FONASA operations is presented in figure 2. Direct fiscal
support to FONASA has fallen almost at the same rate as the
sales of medical vouchers have increased. This trade-off between fiscal support and out-of-pocket payments expresses
the aims and philosophy of the social development model of
the present Chilean government.

PENSION FUND AGENCIES (AFPS)

Chileans who do not place their monthly wage deductions in
prepaid medical group practices or the FONASA can elect
state-insured private pension fund schemes, or annuities,
called AFPs *(administradoras de fondos de pensión)*. Since
1981, the AFPs have accepted monthly wage deductions, and
interest accrues on unused capital. In 1984 the government

approved a plan that would allow AFPs (about twelve) to invest their funds in public firms as risk capital. If this venture proves to be profitable, in several years the AFPs will be able to invest their clients' funds in private firms.[5] According to government officials, profits generated from AFP investment will be high, but there is good reason for skepticism. The November 1981 collapse of the short-lived (1977–81) Chilean "economic miracle" and the high per capita foreign debt suggest that the state is searching for scarce capital in the aftermath of a major monetarist failure. Treasury officials (Ministerio de Hacienda) have privately expressed doubts that the government would be able to fully insure the AFPs should they default (personal communication, Ministerio de Hacienda, 1984).

The Production of Medical Care in Chile

The turn to a market-oriented economy has brought marked changes in how the SNSS budget is allocated. The SNSS delivers medical care to most Chileans—blue-collar workers and indigents. As mentioned earlier, about 58 percent of the population received ambulatory or hospital care from the SNSS in 1977, and about 50 percent in 1983.

Implicit in the shift away from state financing of medical care is the notion that increased medical care budgets (inputs) do not necessarily bring about concomitant improvements in the health status of the population (outputs). In fact, pressure groups in Chile have historically argued the opposite: more resources yield better health (Raczynski 1982; Mesa-Lago 1978; Ochoa 1978). The major changes in the allocation of resources to the main public medical care delivery system in Chile, the SNSS, are outlined in this section. This is the first analysis, to the knowledge of the author, of trends in the SNSS income accounts for the 1962–83 period.

In line with a subsidiary role in the delivery of all goods and services in the public sector, the SNSS replaced the main supplies-purchasing agent, the Central de Abastecimiento

(Central Supply Warehouse), as the only purchaser for public medical programs. Free-market economics dictate that more suppliers of medical care items (medications, medical equipment, beds, etc.) drive costs down. Figure 3 illustrates the relative decline in pharmacy and prosthesis items purchased by the SNSS from the Central Supply Warehouse. Since 1974, private wholesalers have been able to offer some lower-cost items to public hospitals and public clinics. This policy change removed the Central Supply Warehouse from a virtual monopoly (89 percent in 1975) to a supplier of only 40 percent of pharmacy and prosthesis items in 1983. The Central Supply Warehouse now sells to the private sector and has increased its total sales to the private sector from roughly 5 percent between 1974 and 1979 to 14 percent for the 1980–83 period. By opening

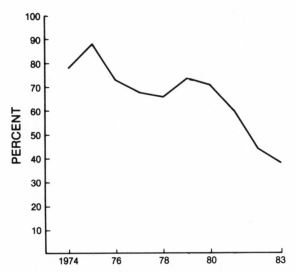

FIGURE 3. *Pharmaceutical and Prosthetic Items Purchased by the SNSS from the Central Supply Warehouse, 1974–83*
Source: Lagos 1984.

itself up to private suppliers, the SNSS, has also purchased more from multinational manufacturers. Imports of foreign manufactured medications and prostheses increased from about 30 percent to 40 percent of the total between 1979 and 1983 (Lagos 1984).

Since 1962, when detailed income statements came into use, the sale of goods and services has never contributed more than 10 percent to the SNSS operating budget (figure 4). Within that 10 percent margin, however, revenues have climbed and fallen according to the health policies of four administrations. This item increased markedly under the conservative government of Jorge Alesandri (1958–64) and during the early years of the liberal Christian Democratic government of Eduardo Frei (1964–70). Subsequently, the Pinochet government increased revenues (i.e., charges to consumers) from medical care, but

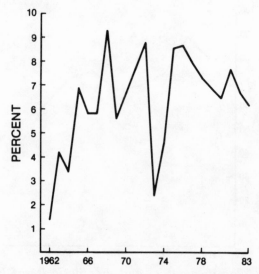

FIGURE 4. *Contribution of Sales of Goods and Services to SNSS Operating Budget, 1962–83*
Source: Compiled from FONASA 1962–83.

again, within the 10 percent margin that characterizes the twenty-one year period.

A breakdown of revenues derived from total goods and services within the SNSS is presented in figure 5. Despite a short period of data unavailability from 1967–71 (due to a change in accounting procedures specified by the General Comptroller's Office), three trends are apparent: (1) the sale of medications contributes insignificantly to revenues, (2) primary care charges have supplied less than 10 percent of all revenues, and (3) vouchers bought under the SERMENA (1972–80) and the FONASA (1980–83) by white-collar middle-class workers have contributed about half of all revenues under the "goods and services" rubric. Thus, of the 10 percent revenues from goods and services in SNSS clinics, about half of the revenues (or 5 percent of the total operating budget) is derived from white-

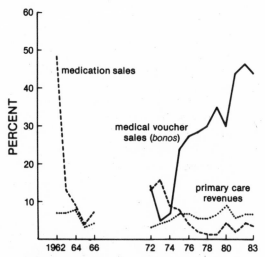

FIGURE 5: *SNSS Revenues from Sales of Goods and Services, by Type, 1962–66, 1972–83*
Note: 1967–71 data were unavailable.
Source: Compiled from FONASA 1962–83.

collar workers who opt for the less attractive facilities of the SNSS. The selection of SNSS clinics by white-collar workers may be due to geographic proximity to work or residence, the attraction of less expensive levels of care (among the multilevel systems of care that characterize SERMENA and FONASA), or the perception that SNSS medical personnel deliver quality care. These possibilities are considered in chapter 4.

A final component of public medical care in Chile is evaluated in figure 6. Turning to the expense side of the SNSS operations, three costs were considered from 1962 to 1983: personnel, pharmaceutical and prosthetic, and real investment. Personnel expenditures (salaries and wages) increased steadily from 1962 to 1973, the years of populist governments, but have declined since 1973. Since the outset of the present regime in Chile, personnel expenses have consumed about 50 percent of total expenses (changes in personnel size are discussed later). Pharmacy costs have nearly doubled since 1974, which is consistent with earlier reports from both Chileans (Belmar et al. 1977) and foreign analysts (Navarro 1974a), who based similar claims on interviews with medical care workers. Finally, real investment (primarily equipment purchases) has been somewhat cyclical but has always remained less than 10 percent of all expenses under all administrations.

In short, trends in selected accounts from income statements from the SNSS suggest four key points in the production of medical care. First, most supplies are now purchased for public medical care on the open market; no longer does the Central Supply Warehouse buy and sell exclusively for the SNSS. Although comparative prices from other private competitors were not considered here, it is assumed that public clinics purchase about 60 percent of their (1984) supplies from less expensive private distributors rather than from the Central Supply Warehouse. A three-fold increase in the producers was noted between 1979 and 1983 and may, in the long run, strengthen the comparative advantages that foreign pharmaceutical firms hold in the Chilean market.

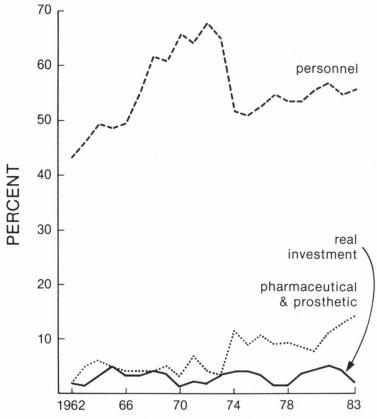

FIGURE 6. *Selected SNSS Expenses , 1962–83*
Source: Compiled from FONASA 1962–83.

Second, less than 10 percent of the SNSS budget has been derived from the sale of goods and services. This percentage has fluctuated in accordance with the medical policies of the four governments in power from 1962 to 1983. These data are at variance with the claim that the poor are contributing significantly to the financing of public medical care in Chile. Clearly, more out-of-pocket charges under the Pinochet government have been levied than during the Allende period; however, the relative contribution of these out-of-pocket charges to the total budget was no greater in 1983 than during the Christian Democratic government of the late 1960s.

Third, the trend in SNSS clinics has been to receive more revenues from former users of the middle-class systems of the SERMENA (until 1979) and the FONASA (1980 to the present). Convenience or continuity of care may account for this crossover to the SNSS, despite the problems of lengthy waiting times, facility cleanliness, and crowding. Finally, personnel expenditures have dropped from a high of 68 percent in 1972 to roughly 55 percent in the 1980s. The trend is consistent with both the retrenchment in total personnel employment by the SNSS between 1970 and 1980 and the purchase of more high-technology medical equipment. This latter move has been the focus of much concern about the concentration of resources and capital equipment in hospitals as opposed to ambulatory care centers (Jiménez de la Jara 1982b).

The Expanding Role of the Private Medical Sector

Free-market approaches in the medical care sector in Chile, while clearly tied to the neoclassical school of economics, are not without precedent elsewhere in Latin America. Brazil has privatized certain aspects of its curative care system in an attempt to spur competition and drive medical costs down. In 1976, 76 percent of Brazil's hospital patients were treated in facilities administered by private management. By 1981, that figure reached 88 percent (Rezende and Mahar 1981). This contractual arrangement in Brazil has allowed the private sector to assume a greater share in medical care delivery, while freeing the public sector of some cost.

INVESTMENT AND EXPENDITURE TRENDS

Public expenditures in the Chilean medical care sector have decreased since 1974 while private expenditures have risen (table 4). Although a disaggregation of the public and private components is not readily available, it is likely that a large part of the increase in the private sector is due to capital purchases. Further refinement of private-sector expenditures is possible through a disaggregation of data from the tax office (Servicio de Impuestos Internos) by facility type (hospital, clinic, group practice, solo practice), but this information is not available to the public.

In keeping with fiscal constraints intended to avoid crowding out private-sector investment, greater losses of revenue, and inflation, the Chilean government signed an International Monetary Fund (IMF) standby agreement in 1984. This agreement stipulates that the nonfinancial public-sector deficit (net government indebtedness and nonfinancial public enterprises) cannot surpass 4.5 percent of the gross domestic product. It has been predicted that the large 1984 fiscal deficit, up from the

TABLE 4
Public and Private Medical Care Expenditures, 1969–70, 1974–80

		Private		Public	
Year	Millions 1980 Pesos	Millions of Pesos	%	Millions of Pesos	%
1969	26,708	14,089	53	12,619	47
1970	27,625	13,557	49	14,068	51
1974	21,666	11,134	51	10,532	49
1975	22,520	12,995	58	9,525	42
1976	23,019	14,210	62	8,809	38
1977	27,141	16,337	60	10,804	40
1978	29,161	18,344	63	10,817	37
1979	29,654	19,036	64	10,618	36
1980	31,709	20,945	66	10,764	34

Source: Viveros-Long 1982, cited in Raczynski 1982, p. 75. Viveros-Long uses data from the Banco Central (Chilean Reserve Board), and private sector earnings are taken from a national sample of private hospitals, clinics, laboratories, medical centers, and physicians.

1983 level of 2.4 percent, will give rise to greater public borrowing from the domestic banking system (U.S. Embassy 1984).

At least two inferences can be drawn about the effect of this borrowing on medical care. First, the nonfinancial debt will likely keep fiscal support for medical care at recent levels or will force budget cuts in order to comply with the IMF repayment schedule. In other words, the downward trend of public funding for medical care (table 4) will probably continue, while private investment increases. Second, and in support of this latter projection, private medical care investment should increase: A report on Chilean economic trends (U.S. Embassy 1984) revealed that medical equipment and instruments are one of nine major investment prospects for U.S. suppliers. Unless consumers now being attended to in public medical programs reduce their demand for medical services, further public retrenchment will send some public users to private providers.

PREPAID GROUP PRACTICES

A main feature of the Chilean government's plan to reduce dependence on state-sponsored medical care has been the stimulation of prepaid group practices as outlined by Law Decree 3626. These new practices, called provisional health institutes (ISAPREs), are similar to the health maintenance organizations (HMOs) in the United States. The cost- and health-effectiveness of HMOs have been well illustrated (Falkson 1981). The organization and financing of the ISAPREs vary from the closed model, typified in the United States by the Kaiser plans, to the less centralized, individual private practices, which enter into service arrangements with licensed medical personnel for the delivery of care on a fee-for-service basis rather than for salaries (Shouldice and Shouldice 1978: 349). Some ISAPREs operate as indemnity carriers, providing claims and payment review, marketing, and management, and assuming risk for subscribers at a given level of care. Thus in a highly structured and authoritarian regime such as Chile's (Caviedes 1984; O'Donnell 1978), the ISAPREs appear to be technical solutions—rather than political solutions—to the perceived need for reducing social spending, a pragmatic view that should enhance the adoption of the ISAPREs by the public (Stone 1980).

Since the passage of Law Decree 3626 in November 1981, employees have been able to place their mandatory monthly medical care withholdings into the ISAPRE of their preference. Subscribers also incur monthly fees and, depending on the level of coverage, pay a portion of curative care charges. In light of the number of payments, therefore, it is not surprising that the ISAPREs are marketed to higher-income groups, those who earn a monthly salary of at least 40 thousand pesos in 1983 (about $500); that is to say, the upper quintile of total wage earners (table 2). The ISAPREs are necessarily selective, owing to their high operating costs. These high-income workers have few dependents and low morbidity risks (Colegio Médico 1981). The location of most ISAPRE facilities, practitioners, and consumers in the high-income neighborhoods of Santiago, Valparaiso, Vina del Mar, and Conception attests to the fact that the ISAPREs seek to recruit upper-income clientele.

Although the performance of prepaid group practices in the United States has been encouraging, the ISAPREs have had less success than originally expected. Since their commencement in 1981 until March 1984, seventeen practices had captured only an estimated 487 thousand beneficiaries (365 thousand unofficially). Furthermore, the three largest ISAPREs have consistently held between 60 and 70 percent of the market share, a percentage that has been gradually declining and may signal the emergence of a more competitive marketplace (i.e., one with more suppliers) in the future (table 5). The growth of the ISAPRE lags far behind the original estimate of a million subscribers in about a hundred practices by the end of 1983 (*La Tercera* 1983, cited in Jiménez de la Jara 1982a; FONASA 1982).

The government's Department of ISAPRE Coordination coordinates medical care delivery and financing in both the public and private sectors. However, although this is a highly recom-

TABLE 5
Enrollment in the ISAPREs, 1982–84

Date	Number of Policies	Number of Enrollees[a]		Number of ISAPREs	% of Largest Three
		Four Persons Per Policy	Three Persons Per Policy		
1982					
September	85,536	255,000	—	10	76.0
October	85,577	255,000	—	11	74.6
November	84,996	255,000	—	11	74.5
December	84,726	254,000	—	11	74.1
1983					
January	84,923	330,000	254,599	11	73.5
February	84,474	337,000	253,253	11	73.0
March	84,809	339,000	254,257	11	71.3
April	85,264	341,000	255,621	11	69.9
May	87,750	351,000	263,075	11	69.4
June	94,019	376,000	281,869	14	66.8
July	96,292	385,000	288,683	14	65.4
August	99,092	396,000	297,078	14	64.6
September	104,071	416,000	312,005	14	74.8
October	108,524	430,000	324,213	14	60.0
November	112,524	440,000	337,374	14	59.0
December	115,412	462,000	346,236	15	58.4
1984					
January	117,997	471,000	353,991	16	57.7
February	120,685	482,000	362,055	16	57.1
March	121,827	487,000	365,481	17	57.6

Source: FONASA, Departmento de Operaciones, n.d., mimeo.
a. In 1983 FONASA changed the estimated number of enrollees per policy from 3 to 4. No public explanation has been given for this change, which increased enrollment by one-third.

mended policy course (Mach 1978; Mesa-Lago 1978), it appears
that the ISAPREs draw patients from FONASA's level-three
care. Public health officials contend that low enrollment in the
ISAPREs is due to the world recession and the low price gar-
nered by Chile's chief export, copper (personal communication,
Ernesto Tupper, 17 October 1983).

Third World countries that uncritically adopt foreign organizational schemes should first ask whether these programs meet
their specific needs (Polgar 1963). A number of ISAPRE managers have consulted with HMOs based in the American Midwest,
where income levels, ethnic composition, and help-seeking
behavior of the population are quite different from Chile's.
Three ISAPREs specifically refuse dependent women (i.e., not
working outside the home) under forty years of age. Still others
require that all women certify that they are not pregnant. These
practices might be culturally acceptable in the United States,
where prepaid medical group practices have evolved. However,
they go against a Chilean tradition of generous maternity care
programs, which have helped place Chile among those nations
with the highest female labor force participation in the formal
sector (Covarrubias and Franco 1978; Meza 1984). In a sense,
therefore, the ISAPREs are anachronistic in Chile because they
demand expensive premiums for women of reproductive age
who work in the home (housewives).

Administrative Change and Medical Policy
Deliberation

To the detriment of medical policy in Chile, there has not been
an open debate on the changes enacted in the last few years. The
experience in Israel, for example, a highly politicized nation like
Chile, shows that public debate on issues of medical care and
social security is a good predictor of program adoption by providers and consumers (Yishai 1982). But the elimination of the
National Health Council Advisory Board as well as the suspen-
sion of the national congress, political parties, and elections

have impeded discussions of proposed medical policy reforms. One Chilean physician and medical services researcher noted that "an unbalanced power is now concentrated in the Ministry (of Health), and health decisions are made by a group of persons designated by a political authority. There is no participation by an autonomous social intermediary nor, of course, does the population affected participate" (Goić 1979a: 560; my translation).

In the past, the Colegio Médico acted as a professional society with legal input in medical policy matters, such as fiscal allocations, fee schedules for ambulatory and hospital care, and administrative boundaries (hospital service districts, clinic districts, and rural medical rounds). This legal relationship changed in 1979 with the issuance of Law Decree 3601, which reduced the legal status of the association to a mere voluntary association. Physicians are no longer required to belong to the Colegio Médico, and information on physician incomes, working conditions, and other data critical to successful medical care planning (Mach 1978) are now more difficult to obtain. Physicians are forbidden to meet in public hospitals and clinics to discuss nonclinical matters. Their input into medical policy is more narrowly represented than ever. At the Ministry of Health, for example, only three of the eight ministers between 11 September 1973 and 1 January 1986 were physicians by training.[6] Information flows from the ministry downward and in this regard is similar to the decision-making structure noted by Ugalde (1978) in his study of other authoritarian governments.

The Colegio Médico has argued that only the state can afford to assume the projected 1983 deficit of $30 million in state-sponsored curative medical care systems. It believes that the move toward market-determined medical prices is undesirable: "The simple game of [market] supply and demand is equivalent to not planning human resources . . . [this in turn] distorts health care professionals, accentuating their power distribution and generating undesirable ethical problems" (Colegio Médico 1983a, no page; my translation).

Physicians also view the move to a market system as the cause of their growing underemployment and unemployment (Colegio Médico 1983b). The proportion of medical graduates hired by the public sector declined three-fold between 1977 and 1982 (table 6). Traditionally, 80 percent of the graduating medical class found work with the state, while the remainder of the class went into full-time private practice, sought specialization abroad, or emigrated (Colegio Médico 1983b).

TABLE 6
Medical School Graduates and SNSS Positions Reserved for Them, 1977–82

Year	Number of Graduates	Number of Positions	Ratio of Positions to Graduates
1977	528	379	71.7
1978	617	321	52.0
1979	676	319	47.2
1980	640	326	50.9
1981	596	153	25.6
1982	662	160	24.1

Source: Colegio Médico 1984.

One revealing trend over the past decade is the increase of nurses, midwives, and medical technologists in the public medical sector (table 7). Substituting such ancillary personnel for physicians is a well-recognized cost-saving measure (PAHO 1982). But long waiting lines and crowded conditions characterize most of the sixty-six public clinics in Greater Santiago and are the result of too few physicians in the SNSS. It is common for lines to form outside clinics several hours before they open (La Segunda 1983, 1984). The underemployment and unemployment of physicians contradicts the apparent shortage of physicians and long waiting lines in Santiago clinics. Augusto Schuster, personal physician to the president and cabinet member of the Ministry of Health, contends that the alleged

TABLE 7
Medical Personnel in the SNSS, 1970–80

| | 1970 | | 1980 | | |
Personnel	Number	Ratio per 10,000 Inhabitants	Number	Ratio per 10,000 Inhabitants	1970–80 Change
Physicians	4,401	4.70	4,128	3.78	−21%
Dentists	1,140	1.22	1,752	1.58	+30
Pharmacists	321	0.34	199	0.18	−47
Nurses	1,666	1.78	2,509	2.56	+51
Physical therapists	174	0.19	360	0.32	+107
Midwives	1,101	1.17	1,839	1.66	+42
Nutritionists	397	0.42	612	0.55	+31
Medical technologists	352	0.38	854	0.77	+103
Other non administrative professionals	1,381	1.47	1,283	0.86	−41
Total or Average	10,933	11.67	13,563	12.20	+5

Source: Modified from Medina and Kaempffer 1982: 1004.

oversupply of physicians is the result of the "university-for-all" policy of the Allende government (Ercilla 1980).

Limited positions in the public sector have forced a growing number of physicians into the private sector. A surrogate measure of this growth is the number of private physicians who advertise in the yellow pages of the Greater Santiago telephone directory. Between 1975 and 1982 there was a 52 percent increase in these listings (Jiménez de la Jara 1982b). This would seem to indicate that the private medical sector in Chile is growing rapidly. However, the number of physicians and their incomes are unknown because the Colegio Médico is restricted in gathering this information (Colegio Médico 1983c). Current disputes between the Ministry of Health and the Colegio

Médico are significant in light of the historical importance that physicians have had in Chilean politics and the design of national medical care policies. Between 1833 and 1973, twenty-one senators and representatives, one vice-president, and one president were physicians by training (Cruz-Coke 1983). Moreover, the Colegio Médico was a catalyst in the formation of the National Health Service in 1952, the Curative Medicine Law of 1968, and in 1973 was one of the first professional organizations to call for the resignation of fellow physician and then president of the republic, Salvador Allende (Chanfreau 1979).

Despite the historical contributions made by physicians and the Colegio Médico in the areas of social legislation, the present government argues that neither the coverage nor the quality of medical care has suffered since the outset of the "modernization" reforms of recent years. The present arrangement, in which the consumer has the right to select freely from among a greater number of systems (both public and private) at various costs, is thought to be the best way to force providers to give better care, to generate competition in the medical marketplace, and to keep costs down (ODEPLAN 1983). The FONASA system illustrates that, while it would be correct to claim that the availability (number of providers) has increased, the accessibility (financial) of primary care has not. As shown in the previous sections, out-of-pocket charges for FONASA patients are now greater in relative and total amounts than they were under its predecessor, the SERMENA.

EVALUATION MEASURES OF HEALTH POLICY

There is a need for measuring the outcomes of the various programs. Little is known about the qualitative aspects of the municipalization program of SNSS clinics or patient satisfaction with FONASA or SNSS delivery systems. Ideally, a medical care bureaucracy as large as Chile's might include a department of research and evaluation. Such operations are costly, however: even the expensive public medical care systems of West Germany and the United Kingdom function without these kinds of departments (Etten and Rutten 1983). One Chilean government evaluation of the municipalization program of SNSS clinics arrived at favorable conclusions about the transfer of clinics to municipal administration without evaluating nonmunicipalized facilities as a control population (which would have allowed statistical inferences to be employed; Ministerio de Salud 1982). Patient satisfaction with SNSS clinics was reported to be very high, but the results and format of the survey (administered jointly by the Ministry of Health and Gallup Chile, Inc.) has not been disclosed (personal communication, Fernando Symon, 4 July 1984; see note 4). Despite the methodological shortcomings of that investigation, it was widely reported among the local news media that consumers of public medical care were highly satisfied.[7]

Government officials argue that the effectiveness of their national health policy is proven by the drop in the infant mortality rate: "Mortality is the most important indicator of quality of life and health" (Ministerio de Salud 1983: 36). On numerous occasions, officials have claimed that the drop in the infant mortality rate (from sixty-five per thousand in 1973 to twenty-three per thousand in 1984) is a direct outcome of their medical care policies. This argument is questionable because (1) infant mortality levels (and many morbidity and mortality indexes) lag several years behind public medical program actions, unless they reflect readily identifiable infectious diseases for which prophylaxis exists; (2) apart from medical care per se, it is extremely complex to sort out those medical versus nonmedical factors that affect infant mortality; (3) no major changes in either the type of infant mortality or the kinds of infant and child medical programs have been noted in Chile since the current government took power in 1973; and (4) vital rates in nations, like Chile, in the last phase of the demographic transition are generally altered by nonmedical factors (McKinlay and McKinlay 1977).

Nevertheless, Racyznski and Oyarzo (1982) found partial

support for a government role in lowering infant mortality. Their multivariate analysis revealed that the rates of state-sponsored primary care checkups of mothers in prenatal and postnatal stages is the variable that best predicted infant survival in Chile. But, as has been documented in the infant mortality literature, infant mortality responds to a multitude of other factors, particularly wage and employment conditions among nonskilled workers in the formal labor sector (Behm 1979; de Carvalho and Wood 1978). Another study of ninety-two public clinics conducted by independent consultants to the Ministry of Health revealed that their maternal and infant care programs were "less than efficient" (Borgoño et al. 1983). The evaluation was based on structural variables such as staff size, materials in stock, organization and management practices, and the adherence to norms and procedures.

The formidable decline of infant mortality levels has led some analysts to speculate that public funds may continue to be reduced should infant mortality remain low (Haignere 1983; Ochoa 1978). Free food supplements for infants and children have been found to be highly correlated with infant survival (Solis et al. 1982; Castillo et al. 1982). On the one hand, the per capita daily consumption of protein was estimated to have fallen from eighty grams in 1972 to sixty-two in 1978 (Mardones-Santander 1981). This decline represents a worsening economy and a decline in consumer purchasing power. On the other hand, the Chilean government has kept distribution levels of these nutritional supplements constant during its fourteen-year tenure.

MORBIDITY AND QUALITY OF LIFE

Other assessments of Chile's medical care policy emphasize nonmedical factors affecting the health status of the Chilean population. Ernesto Medina and Ana Maria Kaempffer, physicians and public health researchers at the University of Chile's School of Public Health, concluded that "the efficiency of medical care has been helped by an increase in the number of people living in urban areas and by the improvement in basic instruction, health education and sanitation" (1982: 1004).

The claim that infant nutrition programs in Chile are determinants of infant mortality decline has been challenged. Hakim and Solimano (1978) argue that, despite popular media support linking infant programs with low levels of infant death, the poor quality of water and storage facilities impedes the efficiency of infant nutrition programs. Moreover, factors other than health policy actions per se (improved female education and water and sewage treatment) during the Pinochet government have helped lower infant mortality. To be sure, infant mortality has not dropped in tandem with the health policy outcomes on a year-by-year basis. There are a myriad of quality-of-life factors that affect infant mortality, and these factors represent the cumulative contribution of health policies, medical care organization, female literacy, and the like.

The quality of health status, therefore, also needs to be assessed by the use of morbidity measures. Alejandro Foxley and Dagmar Raczynski have made this theme a major focus of their study of the social groups vulnerable to the perils of Chile's current economic recession. "Actually, it is a known fact that in nations where the risk of death has diminished constantly and where, in addition, there is a health recovery system covering majority percentages of the population, mortality levels cease to be a suitable indicator of the nation's state of health and susceptibility to disease. In fact, they only reflect the ultimate outcome, that of dying" (1984: 231).

That morbidity is a more pertinent index of the health status of a population is noted by the increase in typhus and hepatitis (figure 7). Infectious diseases of this sort afflicted Chile at a much earlier period of its economic development (Viel 1961). Yet Chile now possesses 25 percent of all typhoid cases in the Western Hemisphere (Colegio Médico 1983a) but has less than 2 percent of the population. Epidemiologists have suggested that the high levels of typhoid fever are attributable to less

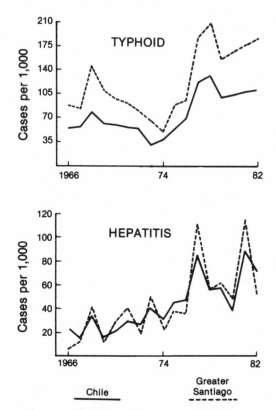

FIGURE 7. Typhoid and Hepatitis Rates, 1966–82
Source: Colegio Médico 1984, p. 34.

frequent inspections of food establishments. During the time when there was an increase in typhus and hepatitis cases in Santiago and the rest of the nation (figure 7), there was also a marked reduction in the number of food inspections by health officials—from 124 in 1974 to only 5 in 1981 (Medina and Yrarrázaval 1983).

Heavy flooding in 1982 and 1983 due to El Niño climatic disturbances partially caused a rise in infectious diseases propagated by contaminated water. During this time the ministries of Public Works and Housing intensified their campaign to "make healthy" (sanear) the squatter settlements of Greater Santiago. Although this process should have entailed connecting homes to the central sewage system (Haignere 1983), raw sewage from the 4.4 million inhabitants in Greater Santiago is still discharged directly into the Mapocho and Maipu rivers without passing through even primary treatment.

Small agriculturalists downstream use this contaminated effluent to produce about 47 thousand tons of such short-cycle vegetable crops as lettuce, cabbage, celery, radishes, and parsley (Servicio Salud Ambiental 1983: 44). Only two officials (from the Environmental Health Service of Greater Santiago) spend only eight hours weekly inspecting the 2,128 hectares of small farms that use contaminated water for field irrigation. When agriculturalists are found using the contaminated water, they are given ninety days to cease the operation (personal communication, Magdalena Iriondo, 27 June 1984). Meanwhile, farmers are allowed to harvest and bring infected crops to market, and some crops, like parsley, are harvested twice in the ninety-day period. Consumers are encouraged to take preventive measures by disinfecting vegetables with a fairly costly commercial chemical, a less-expensive detergent bleach, or soap and water. The Ministry of Health does not subsidize farmers for destroying contaminated crops, even though benefit-cost studies have not assessed the trade-off between cash subsidies and labor productivity losses by workers who are infected by hepatitis or typhus (personal communication, Dr. Fernando Symon, 4 July 1984).

The Faculty at the School of Public Health of the University of Chile recognizes that the government is reluctant to purchase infected crops because of its defined role as a subsidiary agent in social development (ODEPLAN 1983; personal communication, Faculty of the Department of Hospital Administration, May 1984). It is likely that a least-cost preventive strategy of secondary water treatment and crop subsidy would enhance public health.

Summary and Conclusion

The formulation of public health policy and the task of striking a balance between private and public medical care financing are well illustrated by the Chilean case. Providing affordable medical care at an acceptable level of quality, while maintaining fiscal solvency, is a priority in many countries. The private-public medical care debate in Chile has surfaced after sixty years of strong public medical care funding. The evidence reviewed suggests that the private sector will not be able to drive costs down through competition and thereby absorb users from the public sector. The promotion of a market-oriented medical industry in Chile has brought about greater out-of-pocket payments for consumers accompanied by greater incidence of the infectious diseases that afflicted Chile during an earlier period of its economic development.

Redefining the state's role in medical care financing has been accomplished by a number of statutory changes. These changes have allowed the state to relinquish some responsibility in the medical care sector as it breaks its traditional allegiance with the electorate, political pressure groups, and the unions in underwriting medical care services. Employers and middle- and upper-income consumers, mainly, have financed the pension fund schemes (AFPs) and prepaid group practices (ISAPREs); they have also contributed the most out-of-pocket payments. The guiding ideology behind privatizing public services seeks to move back the boundaries of the political apparatus and to return some government duties to the private sector. The case for more out-of-pocket payment rests on the grounds that the government is incompetent in service provision and the traditional welfare state is difficult to manage. Public monies tagged for health care, it is argued, dampen private investment.[8]

Evidence from the first few years of the restructured medical care system point to three main conclusions. First, the expansion of the newly developed private sector is falling short of original estimates. The ISAPREs have captured less than one-third of their projected enrollment figures. Pension monies will soon be invested in dubious state venture-capital operations. Public clinics have been leased to municipal managers in some Santiago municipalities, but a fixed ceiling placed on reimbursements during the first year of the program restricts most municipalized clinics to middle- and upper-income areas.

Second, more careful evaluation of medical policy outcomes is needed so that short- and long-term changes in health levels can be monitored. It is argued here that reductions in infant mortality rates over the last decade are more likely to result from nonmedical factors than from state-financed medical programs. Mortality measures of typhus and hepatitis as well as of water treatment projects and public health campaigns are as important gauges of health status as medical care.

Finally, the fact that Chile has been a pioneer in state-financed medical care will draw attention to the impact of its restructured system. Member nations of the Pan American Health Organization and many Third World countries in Africa and Asia could learn much from careful studies of the Chilean experiment as they, too, deal with external debt problems. Although Chile falls short of meeting the PAHO goal of two medical visits per person annually, it has brought the infant mortality rate below thirty deaths per thousand live births well in advance of the year 2000 goal (El Mercurio 1983b). The Pinochet regime would have a model of medical care administration worthy of emulation among the Third World if the public sector further reduces the proportion of public funds without compromising the quality of life.

III
Inflation and Medical Care Accessibility

The economic crisis of the 1980s has imposed special social costs on all nations, and nowhere has this stress been more acute than in providing affordable medical care. Rising inflation has thwarted efforts to hold medical costs steady. Some analysts have argued that a fiscal crisis afflicts all nations and that the public sector is unable to fill the void where private sector funds cannot or will not be placed (O'Connor 1973). Others remain optimistic about the private sector's ability to create competition under free-market conditions, competition that will ultimately drive medical costs down (Friedman and Friedman 1980).

Little cross-national research has addressed the determinants of medical care inflation—for several reasons. The diversity of administrative and financial structures makes comparison difficult. The proportion of state and private sector funds allocated to medical care varies markedly among nations, thus further impeding international comparisons. A common feature in assessing medical care inflation, however, is the practice of indexing (Feldstein 1983; Jud 1978; Friedman 1974).

One approach in assessing rising costs in national economies is the examination of annual variations in the consumer price index (CPI). The medical consumer price index (MCPI), in particular, allows health researchers to examine the change in purchased medical goods and services over time, thus providing insight into the complex workings of the medical market. One caveat in the use of the MCPI is its failure to keep pace with technological changes and the ensuing revisions in products and services. Another drawback of indexing and MCPI fluctuations is that they represent the *hypothetical* purchase of a basket of medical goods and services as opposed to medical goods and services that are *actually consumed.*

This chapter combines MCPI data from Chile's National Statistics Institute (INE) as well as from two national surveys carried out in 1983. In so doing, it better shows the interrelationship between the hypothetical purchase of medical goods and services and those consumed. The main objectives of this chapter are (1) to measure how the medical consumer's purchasing power (a function of the index of wages and salaries) is related to changes in the Chilean MCPI; (2) to determine whether two major theories of medical care inflation in the United States are pertinent to the Chilean case; (3) to review the major types of medical care expenditures in Chile (primary care, dental care, etc.) and to compare their relative distribution with the weightings allotted them in the MCPI; and (4) to discuss the trends of medical care inflation in Chile in the context of national health policy and to consider its effect on the relative accessibility of medical care.

The first section of the chapter reviews the major factors that contribute to medical care inflation in the industrialized capitalist nations as a backdrop to the Chilean experience. The comparison between Chile and the industrialized nations is not as inappropriate as may seem at first glance. The Chilean medical system has virtually 100 percent coverage through its various state-financed and privately financed delivery systems. Chile has been a pioneer in state-financed medical care throughout most of this century, and only recently has there been a sizeable retrenchment of public monies in the medical sector. A second reason for comparing Chile with the industrialized nations is the paucity of research on medical care inflation in Third World nations, underscoring the need for empirical comparative analyses (Lee and Mills 1983).

The second section traces the evolution of the Chilean MCPI

and CPI over the study period, 1979–83. This time period marks the onset of major changes in the performance of the nation's economy as well as the health policy changes described in chapter 2. The impact of medical care inflation is assessed by means of the real costs incurred by Chileans based on surveys of their consumption of medical goods and services.

Medical Care Inflation in the United States

The rise in the cost of medical care in the United States in the 1970s and 1980s has been well documented. In general, about half of the increase in medical care inflation has been due to price hikes and the other half reflects the combined effect of greater utilization and population growth. The increase in the cost of medical care has moved with rising demand. This combined effect was further exacerbated by greater costs for ancillary services (McCracken 1984).

Medical care inflation in the United States has been described in terms of two general models. The first, demand-pull inflation, contends that consumers attempt to buy greater amounts of medical goods and services than existing supplies. Inflation results when supplies do not increase proportionately. A second interpretation of medical care inflation is often referred to as cost-push inflation. In this context, both wages and input prices increase, forcing greater health care costs to be paid by consumers and third parties. The "fuel" that drives cost-push inflation is often the threat of unionization, which locks wages into automatic cost-of-living adjustments (Feldstein 1983: 234–37; Sorkin 1976).

Because hospitals consume the largest portion of the medical dollar (42 percent) in the United States (*Economist* 1985), most research has focused on hospital performance in the marketplace. Increases in U.S. hospital costs can be attributed to at least three factors. First, since hospitals are labor intensive operations, wage and salary increases must be added to the cost of medical care. When consumer wages increase, greater utilization of medical care is often triggered by consumer choice or by the inducement of additional medical procedures by physicians. Both mechanisms spur higher medical costs when supply fails to respond accordingly.

Second, medical insurance programs dictate reimbursement levels. Hospitals try to keep their costs under these fixed levels so that the differences between reimbursement by third-party providers and real costs can be absorbed by the consumer. Obviously, treating patients at lower costs than levels established by third-party payers (e.g., Medicare's diagnosis-related groups, or DRGs; Medicaid; Blue Cross/Blue Shield; and for-profit private-insurance carriers) signifies profit for the hospital. Finally, the relatively high supply of physicians, especially specialists, affects the total cost. Manpower shortages will drive the cost of medical care up, as will the level of provider specialization. Although physician opposition to physician assistants, midwives, and other personnel has been strong, there is some evidence to suggest that the substitution of ancillary personnel for physicians is cost effective (Kane and Wilson 1977; Record et al. 1980; Lawrence 1978). However, the reluctance of major health insurance carriers to recognize physicians' assistants and nursing practitioners as legitimate providers of medical care has limited their acceptance into the U.S. medical care system (Moscovice 1984; Schweitzer and Record 1977).

Medical Care Inflation in Chile

Chile has long been plagued with high inflation in the national economy. The nation's dependence on a few mineral resources such as nitrates and copper throughout its independence period (post-1833) has left it susceptible to boom-and-bust cycles (Davis 1963). Since the 1950s, Chile, like many of its Latin American neighbors, has been experimenting with indexing (Jud 1978). Indexing allows the performance of the national economy and certain industries to be monitored. The socialist government of Salvador Allende faced a strained economy with an annual inflation rate of 750 percent. Despite efforts by the current regime to dampen inflation, its annual increase averaged 250 percent between 1970 and 1978 (World Bank 1980: 11). For the last twelve years, the Chilean military regime has curtailed social spending, in part, to lower the rate of inflation.

HEALTH POLICY CHANGE AND MEDICAL CARE INFLATION

Health policy has been altered in three significant areas since the current regime siezed power in 1973. First, there has been a sharp reduction in social spending (health, education, housing), which, in the health sector, has meant more out-of-pocket charges. The main middle-class medical program, FONASA, requires more private funds than did its predecessor program, SERMENA.

Second, a major effort has been made to enroll middle- and upper-income wage earners in private, prepaid medical practices, ISAPREs. This change is part of the free-choice system, which has been a central feature of the free-market economy of the current regime.

A third aspect of recent policy changes has been the transfer of public clinics, which generally provide care to indigents and blue-collar workers, to county management. As discussed in the previous chapter, this municipalization process is an effort to reduce state bureaucracy and state-financed care by allowing local authorities to provide care according to the needs of the local community. Primary and secondary care facilities have been turned over to municipal management in selected areas of the country. A private management system now operates the Central Health District of Greater Santiago and is the only one of five districts in Greater Santiago to report a profit in recent years. In brief, the military regime has reduced state-financed medical care while increasing out-of-pocket payments from medical care consumers. These changes portend more efficient medical care supply and utilization.

POSSIBLE CAUSES OF MEDICAL INFLATION IN CHILE

Real income in Chile has declined by 15 percent over the last decade (Cortázar 1983). Within the medical care sector, there has been no threat of unionization, nor have major wage concessions been granted to public health workers. The SNSS employed fewer physicians in 1980 than it did a decade earlier (Medina and Kaempffer 1982). The bargaining power of physicians was greatly reduced in 1979 when the government changed the legal status of the Colegio Médico. Traditionally, the association had legal input into wages paid to all medical personnel. At present, the Ministry of Health and the SNSS set all wage levels.

Figure 8 shows that dentists' and physicians' wages have consumed about the same proportion of the SNSS budget over the last ten years. This trend can, in very general terms, be interpreted as a surrogate measure of all physicians' wages and salaries. Because most Chilean physicians work part time for the SNSS or some public-affiliated medical system, the trend in earning power can be generalized from figure 8. It will also be recalled from the last chapter that both the absolute number of SNSS personnel and public funds in the health sector have declined over the last decade (tables 7 and 4, respectively). Assuming that the increase in physician wages in the public sector mirrors the wages of the physicians in the private sector, it can be argued that physicians' wages have not spurred on inflation. This situation contrasts sharply with inflation in the U.S. medical sector, where physicians' salaries increased by about 200 percent between 1970 and 1980 as a result of increased insurance coverage (Burstein and Cromwell 1985: 65).

A second element of medical care inflation in the United States is the growth of new medical insurance programs such as Medicaid, Medicare, and Blue Cross/Blue Shield. Research suggests that prior to 1983 (the year Medicare implemented prospective payment financing) these third-party financing schemes did little to deter physicians from ordering excessive procedures because of their cost-based reimbursement system.

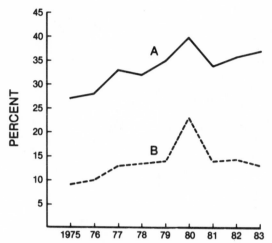

FIGURE 8. *SNSS Physicians' and Dentists' Salaries, 1975–83*
  (A) Defined as physicians' and dentists' salaries divided by all
  salaries and wages. Denominator excludes seniority pay.
  (B) Defined as physicians' and dentists' salaries divided by all
  personnel expenses. Denominator includes wages, seniority
  pay, and bonus pay for accepting rural assignments.
  Source: Compiled from FONASA 1962–83.

In Chile, the major new medical care financing program is
the ISAPREs. To date, these plans have fallen short of their
original goal of one-million subscribers by 1984; as discussed in
the previous chapter, about one-third of that enrollment has
been reached. Even though ISAPRE growth has been slower
than expected, there is no evidence to suggest that it has driven
up private medical care costs (figure 9).

Although new medical insurance programs have not mate-
rialized, the withholding of Chilean wages for medical care
has increased in the 1980s. Monthly wage withholdings are a
major source of medical care financing in Chile. These withholdings are directed to the medical plan of the consumer's
choice. In the context of medical care inflation, it is important
to recall that in 1982 this deduction consumed 4 percent of

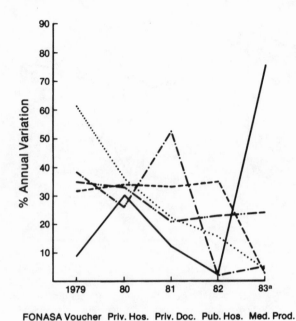

FONASA Voucher Priv. Hos. Priv. Doc. Pub. Hos. Med. Prod.

FIGURE 9. *Annual Variation in Medical Consumer Price Indexes, Selected Items, 1979–84*
a. Denotes December 1983 to March 1984 change only.
Source: INE 1979–83.

gross wages, increased to 5 percent in 1983, and to 6 percent in 1984. These monthly deductions are "purchased," whether or not they are actually "consumed," and are not reflected by the MCPI, thus providing one difference between purchased and consumed medical care.

Finally, it was noted that the use of new medical technology might be responsible for transferring higher costs to medical consumers in the United States, one indication of which is the diffusion of CAT scanners. The Chilean medical market is not yet highly capital intensive. Jorge Jiménez de la Jara (1982a) noted that in 1982 there were only five scanners in all of Chile, and none were in the public sector. I estimate that about ten scanners operated in Chile as of late 1984, of which one was in the public sector.[1] Little evidence suggests that the utilization of medical technology in Chile is likely to be a significant factor in escalating medical care costs, if only because of the scarcity of this kind of equipment.

The data reviewed thus far in the chapter show that the relative price and availability of medical goods and services have increased, particularly in the public sector. The determinants of medical care inflation in the United States are not demonstrated in the Chilean case. Rather, it is hypothesized that the structural causes of medical care inflation in Chile are the result of health policy changes that have shifted more out-of-pocket charges to middle- and upper-income consumers. More empirical evidence for this claim follows.

Methods and Findings

Changes in the MCPI provide only partial insight into medical care inflation. Although the amounts of state and private funds directed to medical care and the rate of inflation are useful data, analyses are confined to generalizations about the hypothetical purchase of certain medical goods and services, as opposed to their actual consumption. To bridge this gap, medical care inflation will be assessed by the performance of the medical care sector and the national economy, as well as by two household surveys on medical care utilization and expenditures among different income and medical program groups.

Trends in the annual change of Chile's CMPI, CPI, and index of wages and salaries (IWS) are shown in table 8 for the 1979–83 period. In the first three years, medical care inflation surpassed national inflation (line 3). These differences reversed in 1982, when the CPI outpaced the CMPI.

The relationship between the CMPI and the IWS was examined to see how medical care inflation compared with changes in the medical care consumer's purchasing power. A

TABLE 8
Medical Care Inflation and Consumer Purchasing Power,
1979–83

Measure	1979	1980	1981	1982	1983
Consumer medical price index (CMPI)	69.45	33.19	23.66	16.52	22.36
Consumer price index (CPI)	38.90	31.20	9.50	20.70	4.00
CMPI − CPI	30.55	1.99	14.16	−4.18	−0.74
Index of wages and salaries (IWS)	53.20	36.54	20.60	5.10	18.00
Ratio of medical care purchasing power (RMCPP) = (IWS:CMPI)	0.766	1.101	0.871	0.309	0.805

Source: INE 1979–83.

ratio of the two measures (wages and expenses) was used to derive an index of medical care purchasing power (IMCPP). This measure is more sensitive than the difference between the CPI and CMPI (line 3) because it relates medical care inflation to consumer purchasing power. The RMCPP (line 5) is calculated following the Laspeyres-type price index; when the index is less than unity (1), the consumer is worse off in the given year (Hirshleifer 1976: 145).

The medical care consumer in Chile was increasingly worse off between 1978 and 1983. The RMCPP shows a gradual worsening in the consumer's ability to keep pace with rising prices in medical services and products. Both an increase in the CMPI and a drop in the IWS made medical care less accessible. A 1983 RMCPP value of 0.805 means that consumers lost about one-fifth of the medical care purchasing power they held in 1978, the base year of the index.

Household survey data from 1983 gathered by the Latin American Institute of Doctrine and Social Studies (ILADES 1984) were used to assess the actual level of medical care expenditures and medical care utilization by income level. Figure 10 shows the proportion of ambulatory care visits for 441 persons in Greater Santiago. A strong and positive correlation is found between the frequency of ambulatory visits and income (Spearman's rank correlation coefficient = .97). This is the expected relationship in economies like the United States, where out-of-pocket payments and insurance coverage are tied closely to income level. The strength of the relationship is unexpected in a country like Chile, where medical care accessibility has not been traditionally hindered by consumer purchasing power. It is consistent, however, with the structure of three-tiered services like FONASA.

To consider medical care expenditures among different private and public medical programs in Greater Santiago, survey results from a Gallup, Chile–University of Chile study were used (Medina n.d.). Table 9 presents the distribution of medical care expenditures for users of various programs (n = 2,820). Total medical care expenditures are shown in proportion to average per capita income as well as to type of care (primary, dental and total care). A striking feature of the data is the high proportion (48 percent) of costs directed toward dental care, disproportionate to the 16.11 percent allocated to this category by the CMPI.

In contrast to the strong correlation between primary care utilization and income data shown in figure 10, no such relationship is apparent between income level and the proportion of income spent on medical care. In this case, Spearman's rank correlation coefficient shows that there is no such relationship at the 95 percent confidence level (table 10). The absence of a strong relationship between income and cash disbursements for dental, primary, and other medical care suggests that other costs — in the form of medical care withholdings and insurance premiums — are at play.

A further refinement in the study of the relationship between real expenditures and medical care programs was sought by selecting those medical programs which represented groups having high, middle, or low income. By focusing on just three medical programs, the differences among income level and

TABLE 9
Per Capita Medical Care Expenditures, by Program, 1983

Program	Income ($)	Medical Care Expenditures ($)[a]	Medical Expenditures as Ratio of Income	Dental Care Expenditures ($)	Dental Expenditures as Ratio of Medical Care Expenditures	Primary Medical Care Expenditures ($)	Primary Care Expenditures as Ratio of Medical Care Expenditures
ISAPRE[b]	1,735	88	5.1	24	27.3	26	29.5
Private doctor	1,061	262	24.7	200	76.3	32	12.2
Doctor friend	1,099	165	15.0	97	58.8	13	7.9
Armed forces	748	427	57.1	104	24.4	16	3.7
FONASA[b]	555	198	35.7	80	40.4	37	18.7
Other pubic program	391	172	44.0	24	14.0	12	7.0
SNSS	189	31	16.4	10	32.3	1	3.2
Average[c]	439	132.5	30.2	63	48.0	14.5	11.0

Source: Income data from Medina n.d., table 5. Per capita income is based on November 1983 levels, at 85.23 pesos to the U.S. dollar. All other data from Medina, n.d. Table 3.
a. Includes primary medical care, hospitalization, pharmacy purchases, and dental care.
b. Excludes monthly payments to public or private program.
c. Medina's survey estimated annual expenditures by "considering real expenditures for the 15 day period [to which all questions referred] . . . and multiplied them by 24" (Medina n.d., p. 39). These averages are unweighted and represent the total sample averages; they are not calculated by separate averages for each medical program affiliation.

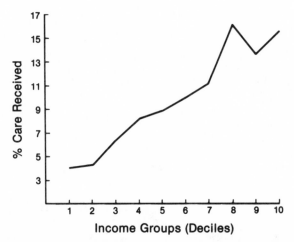

FIGURE 10. *Ambulatory Care Visits, by Income Group, 1983*
Source: ILADES 1984.

medical care expenditures can be emphasized. Private medical care programs (ISAPREs, private doctor, doctor friend), the FONASA, and the SNSS were selected from table 9 to represent the high-, middle-, and low-income groups, respectively. These programs represent approximately 80 percent of all Chilean medical care consumers in the three income ranges, (Scarpaci 1985).

Data were taken from the Gallup–University of Chile study of Greater Santiago (Medina n.d.) on the number of program affiliates who incurred some costs at the time of an ambulatory visit. No measure of the amount of cost incurred was included in the survey. Therefore, I assigned members of the three medical programs to one of two categories: those who incurred some cost and those who did not. A null hypothesis stating there is statistical independence in incurring medical care costs was tested: in other words, incurring medical care costs is not a function of medical program affiliation. A chi-square

TABLE 10
Correlations Between Income and Selected Medical
Care Expenditures

Expenditure	Spearman's Rank Correlation Coefficient
Primary medical care	.643
Dental care	−.452
All medical care	.357

Source: See table 9.
Note: Correlations calculated by author. Significance: $p < .05$.

test measured whether there are significant differences in incurring costs among selected users of these programs (table 11). A chi-square measure of 131.43 from a test of the three groups exceeded the critical level of 13.82 ($p < .001$). Similarly, tests between the FONASA and the SNSS and between the FONASA and the private practices showed significant differences. Thus the null hypothesis was rejected, and the alternative hypothesis, that incurring costs is not random, was accepted. It is concluded that medical program affiliation in Chile, which is closely bound to income level, has some bearing on incurring medical care costs.

Summary and Conclusion

This chapter has combined national-level data from the National Statistics Institute of Chile and two 1983 household surveys of medical care expenditures and utilization in assessing the impact of medical care costs and inflation on consumers in Greater Santiago. At the national level it was found that, although medical care inflation stopped rising faster than the CPI in 1982, wages and salaries failed to keep pace with the prices of medical services and products (CMPI). Medical consumers lost about one-fifth of their purchasing power between 1978 and 1983.

Neither the demand-pull nor the cost-push theories of medical care inflation adequately account for medical care inflation in Chile. Rather, the data analyzed here support the argument that medical care policies in Chile have established the legal framework for the financing of both public and private medical programs, which, in turn, has forced more out-of-pocket payments. The relative cost of medical care increased, while consumer purchasing power fell by about one-fifth from its 1978 levels.

The analysis then turned to realized medical care costs in Greater Santiago. Household survey data from 1983 revealed several important relationships. The utilization of primary medical care is strongly and positively related to income level. This is congruent with the general literature on the utilization of medical services in the United States (Shortell 1980). Moreover, this finding highlights the fact that Chilean medical care policies have shifted toward more personal financing as the state gradually relinquishes its support for medical care. About half (48 percent) of all health care expenditures among those surveyed were for dental care (Medina n.d.). Because consumers in a variety of international settings frequently curtail dental care in times of economic hardship or when other medical needs are pending (Kohn and White 1976), it can be concluded either that latent demand for dental care in Chile is both unmet and strong or that it is a status symbol or a superior good.[2]

TABLE 11
Chi-Square Test of Medical Program Affiliation and Costs Incurred

Medical Programs	Chi-Square	Critical Region	Significance
SNSS, FONASA, private	131.43	13.82	p <.001
SNSS and FONASA	93.23	13.82	p <.001
FONASA and private	79.86	13.82	p <.001

Source: Medina, n.d., table 32, p. 37.

This chapter has measured the differential costs of medical care and medical care inflation in Chile in recent years and its findings underscore the deleterious impact that medical care policies and medical care costs have had on consumers. Unless policy reform shifts the financial and temporal costs from middle- and low-income groups to the state, disparities in utilization will likely widen. This chapter has also demonstrated that medical care is costlier for middle-income users (those who use the FONASA) than for lower-income users (those who use the SNSS) or upper-income users (those who use an ISAPRE). Part of this increased cost for FONASA users is evident from the increases in medical care withholdings from 4 to 6 percent in recent years and from the cost of medical vouchers. Future research should consider the cost of premiums and withholdings in assessing medical care costs in Chile and attempt to determine to what extent consumers "sense" the financial cost of the mandatory withholding of wages.

IV
Help-Seeking Behavior of the Urban Poor

National Health Service System (SNSS) clinics are the first point of entry into the public medical care system. Referrals *(interconsultas)* for secondary and tertiary care are made at this level. For this reason, evaluation of medical care and consumer use at this level is important to understand not only the level of primary medical attention but medical care at higher levels of specialization. Although each SNSS clinic has a designated service area, indigents and *obreros* who lack a regular source of care may attend any facility in the country without financial cost.

The SNSS operated sixty-four primary care facilities in Greater Santiago in 1983. In order to identify consumer satisfaction and use of health care among the urban poor, a representative sample of 140 users of primary medical care was taken from the SNSS-operated Villa O'Higgins primary care clinic in southeastern Santiago (figure 11).[1] The Villa O'Higgins clinic was selected because it provided approximately the metropolitan average of physician hours worked weekly: three female and one male physician each worked there forty hours weekly.

The clinic lies at the periphery of the urban area, as do most low-income districts in Santiago. Clinic users work in occupations common among the urban poor in Chile: government work programs, the informal sector (ambulant vendors, waste recyclers, parking attendants), low-skilled laborers, and domestic servants. La Florida Municipality, where Villa O'Higgins is

69

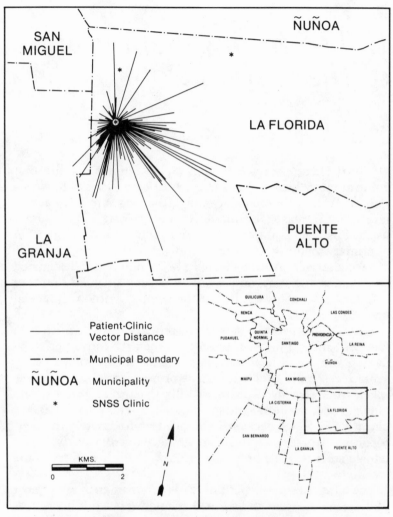

FIGURE 11. Distance Vectors Between Patients' Residences and the Villa O'Higgins Clinic

located, is well served by a public transportation network for intramunicipal and intermunicipal travel.

The author administered a questionnaire to 140 users of the Villa O'Higgins clinic after they had met with one of the clinic's four primary care physicians. (See appendix A for a list of the variable labels and a brief definition of each; appendix B for the original, Spanish-language questionnaire; and appendix C for the English-language translation.) Patients were told that the interviewer was not affiliated with the SNSS. The questionnaire was administered in the Chilean spring (November 1983), a season when the weather is moderate and its influence on health is minimal (Medina, n.d.).

Villa O'Higgins's Patients

DEMOGRAPHIC PROFILE

Of the patients interviewed in this survey, 73 percent were female; a quarter were mothers who had brought their children in for medical examinations. None of the patients sought contraceptives or family-planning counseling, as these functions are handled in another section of the facility during certain morning hours. The population was middle-aged ($M = 35$).

Patients came from large and poor households that spend most of their income on food. These households were on average larger (5.0 versus 4.6) than the municipal mean (Municipality of La Florida 1984). A household monthly income average of 8,200 pesos (about $100) revealed that most families fell below an often-cited, although unofficial, poverty level of 12 thousand pesos (*El Mercurio* 1983c). Three-quarters (76 percent) of household income was spent on food, a disproportionate amount compared to the 42 percent of the consumer price index that measures food price changes in Chile (INE 1983). This large outlay for food may account for the consumers' dependence on the clinic for most of their prescribed drugs, which are free.

Household monthly income showed a moderate and positive

correlation with the number of men (.38) and women (.28) ($p < .001$) working outside of the home.[2] Per capita income was negatively related to the presence of children five years old or younger in households ($-.31$), the need to find child care when adults attend the clinic ($-.29$), and waiting time at the clinic ($-.31; p < .001$). The relationship between waiting time and per capita income concurs with comments made to the author that auxiliary staff give preferential treatment to better-dressed patients and that some consumers are able to pay people to wait in line for them as early as 4:30 A.M. until the numbers for the queue are allotted at 7:30 A.M.

The expected positive relationship between the number of working adults in the household and income levels was found. Almost one-third (29 percent) of all households lacked adult male workers and were accordingly classified as female-headed households (FEMHEAD). The FEMHEAD variable exhibited the expected relationships with the number of working men ($-.53$), working women (.40), and men in the informal ($-.27$) and formal ($-.32$) sectors of the economy ($p < .001$). Differences in employment were found between the sexes. Government work programs were the greatest source of employment for men, whereas the informal sector provided the main source of income for women. Nearly twice as many men (19.8 percent) as women (11.8 percent) were unemployed.

Compounding the economic pressures brought on by unemployment was a high dependency ratio of 2.2 unemployed household members (unemployed adults, children, retirees, students) for each wage earner. Twenty-two percent of the homes had pensioned retirees. Working outside of the home was also different for men and women. While nine out of ten households had at least one male who worked outside the home, only 58 percent of the households had women who worked outside the home. Given this gender difference, it is not surprising that household income was slightly more strongly correlated with the number of working women (.37) than with working men (.28; $p < .001$).[3]

One measure of the well-being of the patients' neighborhoods (PERPOOR) was taken from an ongoing government survey.[4] The range of the percentage of neighborhood residents who were poor was from 6 percent to 25 percent, with a mean of 18.7 percent ($SD = 3.6$). The PERPOOR variable was moderately correlated ($-.36$, $p < .001$) with the distance-to-clinic variable (KILOM), attesting to the relatively good location of the clinic.

HEALTH PROFILE

Patients interviewed at Villa O'Higgins had much experience with health care providers in both the public and private sectors. Nearly all (95 percent) had been treated at the first-aid station *(posta)* and 74 percent had been hospitalized at least once.[5] Slightly less than half (46 percent) of the patients had seen a private doctor either because they had medical coverage or once had money to see one (48 percent), needed to see a specialist (31 percent), or required urgent care (17 percent).

Acute care patients comprised 66.4 percent of the sample and the rest were chronic-care patients for such treatment as diabetes, high-blood pressure, and alcoholism. Leading illnesses within the last two years for the chronic-care patients were pulmonary diseases (24 percent), degenerative diseases (15 percent), nonpulmonary infectious diseases (12 percent), and diabetes (9 percent).

The use of modern versus traditional medicines was addressed by the questionnaire. Prescription and nonprescription drugs are sold in pharmacies in Chile, and one-third of those interviewed relied on the pharmacy as a regular source of medication or advice. Clerks, managers, pharmacists, and even shoppers in Chilean pharmacies frequently give health care advice. Herbal remedies are widely sold by street vendors and shopkeepers. Traditional medicines are more prevalent among Villa O'Higgins's patients than modern pharmaceuticals: more than half (59 percent) used herbal remedies in the form of teas, unguents, and purges, while only about a third (36 percent) used the pharmacy regularly.

USE OF CLINIC

Most patients (70 percent) interviewed had been using the Villa O'Higgins facility for the last five years, and a small percentage (20 percent) had changed facilities just once in that same period, implying that the user population was fairly stable.

When patients were asked if they always came to the clinic when they were ill, 85 percent answered affirmatively, suggesting that they depended heavily on the medical care at Villa O'Higgins. Reasons for attending Villa O'Higgins were that they felt they had a right *(me corresponde)* to use the clinic (44 percent), that it was the closest clinic (33 percent), that they lacked medical coverage (10 percent), and that the care at the clinic was good (10 percent).[6]

One measure of use is the frequency of visits in the last year (FREQVIS). Patients interviewed averaged 6.4 visits per year, with a range of one to thirty visits (SD = 6.4).[7] Unexpectedly, a chi-Square test revealed no significant differences between the frequency of visits among chronic and acute care patients. This lack of expected correspondence may be attributable to the large number of mothers who brought their children to the clinic, thereby increasing the number of visits by acute care patients. One-quarter (24.3 percent) of all patients were visiting the clinic for the first time, and 15 percent had attended at least twelve times in as many months.

Most patients passing through the clinic received a prescription drug or laboratory test. Eighty-five percent of the patients were given drugs from the clinic pharmacy during this visit to the clinic. About one-third of the patients had a laboratory test or examination prescribed at the clinic or the public hospital five kilometers away.

Three questions examined potential hindrances to clinic use as a result of the patient's job obligation, household responsibilities, and the administrative structure of the clinic. The first question showed that two-thirds came to the clinic as soon as they became ill or noted symptoms and were attended. Of the third who did not receive care at the onset of illness, the reasons were "came but was not attended" (19 percent), "took home remedies; sickness worsened" (14 percent), and "work problems" (4 percent). That one of five patients returned because they were not attended on previous visits (either because they tired of waiting or could not be seen) would indicate a shortage of medical personnel. Although only 4 percent delayed in seeking care because of work problems, it is important to note that all Chileans who work in the formal sector are exempted from work for the purpose of a medical visit. Notably, those workers who delayed in seeking care were informal-sector workers.

The second question showed that child care concerns did not form a major hindrance to clinic use. Half of those surveyed had no children in the home. For those who had children in the home, significant others (friends, neighbors, spouse) watched the children in 35 percent of the cases, 14 percent said that the children looked after themselves, and 11 percent brought the children to the clinic. Thus, although three-quarters of the interviewees were female, child care was not a barrier to seeking medical assistance.

A third question assessed possible barriers to clinic use by asking "what difficulties did the clinic place on you to get care." Two out of three patients (68 percent) claimed they experienced no clinic-related difficulties. The chief clinic-related problem was that the social workers or auxiliary personnel (who assign patients to queues) were discourteous. Patients and staff contend this conflict usually centers on whether or not the patient has an alternative source of care or is indigent. One-quarter of all patients had to show either an SNSS medical care provision card (15 percent) or a residency certificate from the Villa O'Higgins service area (9 percent). Requesting a certificate of residency is not a required procedure, since all persons without employer-sponsored care may be attended at any SNSS facility.

The clinic requested partial payment for drugs or tests from only two persons (1.5 percent). Thus the majority of patients felt that the clinic did not impede care.

Geographic barriers in the form of geometric (linear) distance and travel time to the clinic were not major deterrents for patient use of Villa O'Higgins. Half the patients lived within 0.7 kilometers of the clinic (SD = 0.86), and about two-thirds (62.1 percent) reached the clinic in ten minutes or less (M = 13.73, SD = 12.29). All but two patients came from the La Florida Municipality, even though the clinic is located close to municipal boundaries (figure 11). Because patients' medical indigence is certified by La Florida social workers, it is likely that patients can be more easily treated in that municipality.

Patients overwhelmingly (85 percent) said they lived close to the clinic and nearly the same proportion (86 percent) walked there. Travel costs were incurred by 9 percent, who traveled by bus (96 percent) and automobile (4 percent). Patients' perceptions of their proximity to care (PROXIM: 1 = close, 0 = far away) are corroborated by their correlations with the distance-to-clinic variable (−0.42) and by patients' estimation of travel time (−0.39; p < .001). Median travel time was nine minutes, and the mean was about fourteen minutes.

SATISFACTION WITH CLINIC

Patients were asked open-ended questions concerning their single greatest dislike and like about the clinic. On the one hand, half (49 percent) the people interviewed did not express a dislike. Those who had dislikes cited especially lengthy waits (24 percent), poor treatment by the staff (19 percent), and lack of cleanliness in the waiting area and restroom (5 percent). On the other hand, four of five had something good to say about the clinic. Eighty-three percent of the patients cited a physician-related factor (the doctor touched them, listened attentively, etc.) as their greatest like.

A common feature in state-run primary care centers around the world is the inordinate waiting time between arrival and examination. It was not surprising, therefore, to find a 4.2 hour mean waiting time (SD = 1.95).[8] Unpredictably, however, there was no relationship between waiting time and expressed quality of care. This lack of correspondence may be because younger family members often wait in line for older family members in order to get a number for the queue for the limited number of daily examinations.

Lastly, the questionnaire posed three questions that examined patient views on the continuity of care. Sixty percent of the respondents said that physicians are rotated too often. Despite the alleged turnover of doctors at the clinic, half (51 percent) of the patients said they were able to select the physician of their choice. All 140 patients said that they preferred to be examined by the physician of their choice.

Levels of patient satisfaction were measured by two variables. The variable EASECARE was coded as a dichotomous variable for the following question: "Was it easy or difficult to get care at the clinic?" Responses were coded 1 = easy and 0 = difficult. Nearly two-thirds of all patients (64 percent) said that it was easy to get care. The EASECARE variable was correlated with other dichotomous variables: CLINLIKE (specification of a single like, .31, p = .0001); travel time (TRAVTIME, −.25, p = .0034); and whether or not respondents offered any suggestions when asked what improvements could be made to increase the efficiency of the clinic (SUGGEST, −.39, p < .001). The correlation between the ease with which care was obtained and making a suggestion indicates that suggestions were given mainly when it was difficult to get care.[9]

A more refined outcome measure of care (QUALCARE) was coded from responses to the following question: "Would you say the medical care was very good, good, fair, bad, or very bad?" Care was generally well perceived, as shown by the responses: very good (12.1 percent), good (72.1 percent), fair (14.3 percent), bad (1.5 percent), and very bad (0 percent).

The QUALCARE variable was moderately correlated with other dichotomous variables (table 12). Despite the relatively

TABLE 12
Selected Correlates of Quality of Medical Care
(QUALCARE)

Variable	Correlation Coefficient	Significance
KIDCARE	−.22	.0103
CLINLIKE	.34	.0001
DISLIKE	−.21	.0117
HOSPITAL	−.26	.0024
GOODCARE	.26	.0018

Note: Responses were coded 1 = yes and 0 = no. See Appendix A for variable definitions.

low correlations, the relationship is significant given that the variables in table 12 are qualitative variables (binary), and thus it is more difficult to produce good linear fits from them; there is also less than a 2 percent chance that the relationships are the result of unrepresentative sampling. The variables CLINLIKE (e.g., liked the physicians, the receipt of a drug) and DISLIKE (e.g., disliked crowded conditions, long wait, staff treatment) correlate with QUALCARE in the expected directions. The significance of the HOSPITAL variable is more difficult to decipher, given that about three-fourths of the patients were hospitalized at least once. Only the GOODCARE variable, which measured whether or not the doctor examined the patient well (asked questions, touched and talked with the patient, showed interest in the patient), specifically measures the physician-patient relationship.

Predictors of Patient Use of and Satisfaction with Medical Care

This section presents the results of two multivariate models in predicting types of help-seeking behavior. One model is comprised of demographic variables, the other organizational variables (table 13). These demographic and organizational models

TABLE 13
Variables of Demographic and Organizational Models

Variable	Definition
Demographic Model	
ABLEMEN	males over 14 not studying
ABLEWOM	women over 14 not studying
AGE	age of patient
FEMHEAD	female-headed household
FEMINFOR	women in informal sector
FOODPER	food expenditures per person
HHSIZE	household size
KIDCARE	child-care concerns
LIFCYC	presence of children under 5
MENINFOR	number of men in informal sector
MENSTDNT	number of men over 14 studying
MOMKID	mother bringing child for care
PEMMEN	male worker in state program
PEMWOM	female worker in state program
PERCAP	per person household income
PRIVDOC	ever attended by private doctor
SEX	gender of patient interviewed
TIMEILL	chronic- or acute-care patient
WOMSTDNT	adult female students
WORKRATE	adult workers/all adults
Organizational Model	
CLINCAMB	clinic changes in last 5 years
DRUGTEST	receipt of drug or test cited as reason for quality of care
DOCSELEC	able to see preferred doctor
GOTDRUG	receipt of drug or test at clinic
KILOM	vector distance, home to clinic
PERPOOR	percent poor in users' neighborhood
PROXIM	lives close to or far from clinic
STAFCAMB	thought staff changed a lot
TRAVTIME	travel time to clinic
WAITIME	waiting time at clinic
WHYDELAY	reason for delay in seeking care

of care attempt to select the best predictors of the frequency of medical care utilization and consumer evaluation of that care.

Demographic variables (family size, life cycle, age, and gender) are fixed and thus are not easily changed by administrative intervention. However, they are useful in identifying group needs. Organizational variables measure procedures performed on patients, factors that influence their waiting and travel time, ecological conditions of users' neighborhoods, and their spatial behavior in seeking care. Unlike the demographic model, the organizational model is subject to policy or administrative intervention (Shortell 1980: 67).

USE OF CARE

Three independent variables thought to be predictors of the number of visits to the clinic in the last year were graphed against the FREQVIS variable.[10] Interaction was tested between travel time and linear distance from home to clinic (TRAVTIME, KILOM). A general linear model was then used in selecting the best predictors of the frequency of visits to Villa O'Higgins in the last year. Six variables explained 26.8 percent of the model variance (table 14). The significance of the F-value and the R-square led to the rejection of the null hypothesis. In turn, the alternate hypothesis, stating that at least one of the model coefficients is nonzero, was accepted (Benson and McClave 1982: 474).

A series of regression trials produced six independent variables in its best model: half were organizational variables and half were demographic. Taken as a whole, the independent variables predict that the most frequent users are mothers with children who live relatively close to the clinic. The model is appealing in that nearby residents (mostly mothers) with children under the age of five would be expected to attend more often since their health status is likely to be the most precarious. As experienced users, parents would be more familiar with clinic operations, thereby waiting less time. Because a limited number of appointments are provided one day in ad-

TABLE 14
Predictors of Clinic Use (FREQVIS)

Source	DF	Sum of Squares	Mean Square	F	Probability > F
Model	6	25.925	4.321	5.251	0.0001
Error	86	70.801	0.823		
C total	92	96.726			

Root mean sq. error 0.907				R-square	0.268
Dependent Mean	6.429				

Variable	DF	Parameter Estimate	Standard Error	T for H: PARAM. = 0	Probability
INTERCEPT	1	1.490	0.277	5.37	.0001
MOMKID	1	0.819	0.221	3.71	.0004
LIFCYC	1	0.288	0.213	1.35	.1790
TRAVTIME	1	0.012	0.013	0.90	.3697
WAITIME	1	−0.100	0.051	−1.95	.0546
TIMEILL	1	−0.001	0.006	−0.17	.8619
TRAVTIME* KILOM	1	−0.173	0.007	−2.32	.0229

Note: See Appendix A for variable definitions.

vance, it is likely that those who live closer to the clinic would have greater access to making an appointment. Patients or their designates must appear at the clinic to secure an appointment with the physician, because patients cannot schedule appointments at SNSS clinics by telephone. Chronic versus acute patients (TIMEILL) were not significant predictors of utilization, as suspected.

SATISFACTION WITH CARE

Two dependent variables addressed patients' satisfaction with care. The first of these variables, QUALCARE, was best predicted by four independent variables (table 15) that explain about 30 percent of the total model variance. Variables GOODCARE and

TABLE 15
Satisfaction with Medical Care (QUALCARE)

Source	DF	Sum of Squares	Mean Square	F	Probability > F
Model	4	13.227	3.3070	14.207	0.0001
Error	135	31.424	0.2328		
C total	139	44.650			

Root mean sq. error	0.482	R-square	0.2962
Dependent var. mean	2.950		

Variable	DF	Parameter Estimate	Standard Error	T for H: PARAM. = 0	Probability
INTERCEPT	1	2.151	0.144	14.894	.0001
DISLIKE	1	0.394	0.138	2.864	.0049
GOODCARE	1	0.622	0.117	5.308	.0001
DRUGTEST	1	0.712	0.146	4.892	.0001
LIFCYC	1	−0.177	0.082	−2.168	.0319

Note: See Appendix A for variable definitions.

DRUGTEST show that good medical care (i.e., physician chair-side manner and receipt of a drug or test, respectively) is the best predictor of perceived quality care. Patients from younger households presumably use more medical care for pediatric purposes than other patients, and this variable (LIFCYC) therefore enters the model. Except for the LIFCYC variable, all of the significant independent variables are organizational variables.

The EASECARE variable was used as a dependent variable for several reasons. Although the measure is a dichotomous measure of whether care was easy or difficult to obtain, it is pertinent to the SNSS consumer. The binary variable shows no graduated response scale but can, at a very general level, point to trends about cultural and organizational aspects of medical care accessibility. It will be recalled that nearly three-quarters of the respondents said that the quality of care was "good." That many described care as "good" might indicate politeness by the interviewee, fairly consistent treatment of all patients at the clinic, or a combination of these factors. Thus the EASE-CARE measure complements the regression results of the QUAL-CARE variable.

A logistic procedure was used because it fits a regression-like procedure to models with binary (0 or 1) dependent variables (SAS 1982). Unlike standard multiple regression procedures, which use ordinal or interval measures as dependent variables, logistic procedures lack standardized partial regression coefficients and *R*-square measures. One way to interpret the results of logistic regression is the use of predicted proportional effects (Henretta and O'Rand 1980; Nerlove and Press 1973). Predicted proportional effects are the predicted changes in the probability of gaining easy access to care, which results from a unit change in the independent variables when the respondent would otherwise be predicted to be at the mean of the dependent variable (i.e., when patients would have a fifty-fifty chance of finding easy access to care; Petersen 1985).

The logistic regression results, like the standard multiple regression models for FREQVIS and QUALCARE, indicate that organization variables based on residential and patient-at-clinic attributes are the best predictors of care. The KILOM, PERPOOR, and TRAVTIME variables contribute 12.4 percent, 2.9 percent, and 1.6 percent, respectively, to the total predicated proportional change (table 16). The logistic regression results

TABLE 16
Predictors of Medical Care Accessibility (EASECARE)

Variable	Logit Coefficient	Chi-square	Probability	Predicted Proportional Change
KILOM	.5304	2.46	.1171	.1237
PERPOOR	.1268	3.57	.0590	.0297
TRAVTIME	−.0698	9.91	.0016	.0163

Note: See Appendix A for variable definitions.

imply that individuals traveling from more distant neighborhoods report more difficulty in receiving care. This relationship is in accordance with the relative location of the clinic; the proportion of poor neighborhoods decreases as distance from the clinic increases.[11]

Discussion and Summary

The findings at the Villa O'Higgins clinic lend themselves to review within both a national and international context of medical services research. At the national level, this study confirms a finding of a survey sanctioned by Chile's Ministry of Health and the SNSS that a "high degree" of satisfaction exists among users of public medical care (El Mercurio 1984c). The Villa O'Higgins study, however, shows that patients distinguished visits with doctors from administrative procedures. It is also apparent that users view care in very pragmatic terms or that they lack experience in medical programs with shorter waiting times. The inherent problems of long waiting lines (averaging 4.2 hours), conflict with ancillary personnel, and an overall lack of clinic amenities are offset by good physician treatment.

No significant differences in the levels of use or the degrees of satisfaction were found between users from female- versus male-headed households, despite some evidence to the contrary noted by Raczynski and Serrano (1984) in their study of a low-income neighborhood in northern Santiago. However, about one-third of the female users in this study depended on significant others for child care when they attend the clinic. This integral social network of help and reciprocity is an important element among the urban poor throughout Latin America (Lomnitz 1978; Schmink 1982).

Possibly, the economic homogeneity of the sample population accounts for the lack of significant differences among income groups in the perception of care and the frequency of use. There is no comparative figure to assess the significance that one-third of the sample found care to be generally inaccessible at Villa O'Higgins. That 19 percent of the users previously could not get care indicates a shortage of physicians. The number is greater if those that do not attend because of the perception of a long wait are considered.

A major health care survey in Chile was carried out within one month of the Villa O'Higgins study. Physician and public health researcher Ernesto Medina (n.d.) coordinated a study of 604 families (2,820 persons) carried out in Santiago by Gallup Chile, Inc. The research focused on the utilization patterns, morbidity profiles, and socioeconomic characteristics of users among eight public and private medical care programs in Santiago. Medina computed an optimum measurement of care shown in table 17. Weighted scores were given to responses very good (7), good (6), fair (3), and deficient (1). The optimum percentage (100 percent) is compared to the actual responses multiplied by their respective weights. Responses from the QUALCARE variable at Villa O'Higgins are compared to the Medina study. "Bad" and "very bad" responses from the Villa O'Higgins were classified as "deficient" for comparative purposes.

Villa O'Higgins patients had a more positive appraisal of their medical care than the SNSS and "other public" groups, but they were less satisfied than their counterparts in the pri-

TABLE 17
Patients' Ratings on Quality of Medical Care, 1983

Rating	SNSS	Villa O'Higgins	All Public	All Private
Very good	11%	12%	15%	48%
Good	65	72	66	52
Fair	17	14	14	0
Deficient	8	2	5	0
Optimum	72	82	78	92

Source: All data except those for Villa O'Higgins are from Medina n.d., table 29.

vate sector. This positive view of medical care given by the
SNSS contrasts markedly with patients' outlook on life. The
SNSS users were much less satisfied with their lives than users
from other medical programs (table 18). The Villa O'Higgins
survey did not ask a similar question, but it is likely that users
would respond like those of other SNSS clinics, given their
similar economic backgrounds. Physicians who listen, examine, and touch the patient provide support in the difficult and
stressful life of the urban poor. Future research should examine
this relationship between the perception of medical care and
its role in the general state of patients' well-being.

Consumers' preferences for private versus public medical
care in this study have policy implications. Users clearly preferred public providers over private ones, even if they had the
expendable income to seek care from the private sector. Fifty-

TABLE 18
Patients' Responses on Outlook on Life, 1983

Patient's Medical Program	Satisfaction with Life		Quality of Life		
	Satisfied	Unsatisfied	Good & Very Good	Fair	Bad & Very Bad
SNSS	30%	70%	11%	48%	41%
Military	71	29	60	33	7
Other public	37	63	19	71	10
FONASA	51	49	42	43	14
ISAPRE	64	36	66	28	3
Private (solo)	64	36	49	44	6
Private (clinic)	62	39	48	30	22
Physician friend or relative	61	39	32	47	16
Average[a]	55	45	40	43	24

Source: Medina n.d., table 23, p. 27.
a. These averages are unweighted and represent the total sample averages;
   they are not calculated by separate averages for each medical program affiliation.

five percent of the respondents had never seen a private physician, and nearly the same percentage (53 percent) preferred to see a public doctor as opposed to a private one. The leading response among those who preferred private medical care was that it was quicker (58 percent), followed by those who thought it was better than public care (17 percent).

A related variable (IFBUCS was then measured by responses to, "If you had more money would you prefer to see a private physician? " Only 52 percent of the respondents answered affirmatively. A strong and negative relationship (−.90) between the preference for a private doctor (PREFPRIV) and the desire to use private physicians if money were no barrier (IFBUCS) indicates that SNSS consumers' demand is very inelastic. Patient satisfaction with SNSS-delivered care may be due in good measure to the fact that medical care is free and few alternatives exist.

As the Chilean government gradually withdraws public funds from the total medical care system, the poor will be most affected. Moreover, the possible implementation of across-the-board small charges for SNSS services and medical products (Spoerer 1973) will likely reduce utilization. Because only about one-fourth of household income remains after food expenditures, medical care costs would then have to compete with needs such as housing and clothing. If superfluous medical care exists, then perhaps fewer trips to the clinic would not affect the population's health status.

Related to consumer satisfaction in public-sponsored primary care is the high percentage (85 percent) of patients who received a prescription drug. This variable (GOTDRUG) did not correlate significantly with any outcome measures, perhaps because so many patients receive drugs that it has become routine at this clinic. Moreover, patients preferred expensive imported medications over national brands.[12] Urban consumer preference for imported medical care items was also noted in a study by Zalazar (1983a; 1983b) of 196 low-income residents in southern Santiago. As is true for rural medical care users in

Chile, the use of herbal remedies in Santiago complements modern medication and does not act as a substitute for it (Scarpaci 1983).

Spatial variables proved to be antecedents to the outcome measures assessed. Distance and travel time to the clinic have been important in other medical care settings as well (Shannon et al. 1969). Bice and White's review of the World Health Organization's survey of cross-national patterns of medical care utilization concluded that "the use of physicians' services decreases . . . with increasing distance to physicians. Regardless of income bracket, the use of physician services is distinctly greater among persons living near a physician than among other distance groups . . . the effect of distance seems to be linked chiefly to persons of small income" (1971: 254).

Kohn and White (1976: 50) documented in their review of the same WHO study that 77 percent of all patients lived within fifteen minutes of the clinic. A 1969 national survey in the United States revealed that 49.7 percent of the population could get to their regular source of primary medical care in less than fifteen minutes (Aday and Andersen 1975). Users of Villa O'Higgins have comparable, if not slightly better, geographic access than users in other medical care settings.

Survey findings here lend themselves to further direct comparison with international studies of physician use. In general, there is a strong relationship between the receipt of an "objective" medical treatment, such as an X-ray, laboratory test, or prescription drug, and the perception of high quality medical care (Donabedian 1980: 39), a correlation also borne out in this study by the presence of variables GOODCARE and DRUGTEST in the final regression model, with QUALCARE as the dependent variable.

Cultural differences in beliefs about the composition of good medical care are highlighted by this study and a seminal British study of general practitioners in England and Wales conducted by Ann Cartwright (1967). Using open-ended responses,

Cartwright asked British patients to identify the attributes of general practitioners that they appreciate. None of the British respondents said that being touched by the physician was an important attribute.[13] In contrast, touching was frequently cited by Villa O'Higgins patients as a reason why care was good (coded by the GOODCARE variable). Thus Freidson's (1961) contention that all patients want both "competence" as well as "personal interest" from their providers is supported in the present study, but "personal interest" is culturally determined.

The variance explained by the models used in this study show remarkable consistency with other studies (see Mechanic 1979). In the United States it appears that more than 85 percent of all users are satisfied with medical care, mainly because they have medical providers whom they feel are good (Roemer 1980: 377). Feldman (1966) concluded that 89 percent of U.S. patients surveyed were "entirely satisfied" with care, and only 11 percent were "not entirely satisfied." A 1975–76 national study of U.S. patients found that 88 percent were satisfied with their last visit to the doctor and 87 percent were satisfied with the quality of care (Robert Wood Johnston Foundation 1978). In the Villa O'Higgins study, satisfaction per se was not measured, but it can be approximated by collapsing the responses to QUALCARE. "Very good" and "good" responses accounted for 84 percent of all evaluations, again coinciding with the trend found in the general literature.

Also in harmony with the literature is the percentage of model variance explained in the analysis of quality of care and utilization. Shortell (1980: 78) has shown that models of utilization at modern medical settings tend to explain from 15 to 25 percent of the total variance. Mechanic (1979: 388) says that the explained variance ranges from 16 to 25 percent. Wolinsky (1978), for example, predicted physician utilization with regression models using twenty-nine predictors. These independent variables explained between 9 and 12 percent of the variance. That models of utilization and satisfaction tend to explain relatively little variance may be the result of measurement or specification error, or there may be little variation in the dependent variable due to a halo effect in responses. This study was able to explain 26.8 percent and 29.6 percent of the variance in the FREQVIS and QUALCARE variables, respectively.

Institutional access to primary medical care for women and those from female-headed households appears to be better in Chile than in other Latin American countries, according to this study. Because of the national coverage provided by the SNSS, program affiliation in a particular pension or social security program is not required to receive primary medical care in Chile. In Colombia, women have less access to social security benefits, which in turn limits their use of primary care. This gender difference reflects the fact that more men work in the formal sector, where medical care coverage is available (Tellez 1977). Differential access to social security benefits is also a problem in Lima, where almost 88 percent of the manual workers eligible for medical care are men (Urrutia 1975). A study in Belo Horizonte, Brazil, found that female-headed households are twice as likely to use charitable or church-sponsored medical services as government-sponsored programs (Schmink 1982). This is common throughout Latin America, because greater numbers of women work in the informal sector, where medical care benefits do not exist (Schmink and Merrick 1982). These studies all demonstrate that organizational settings greatly affect patterns of medical care.

Part of the inherent difficulty in comparative medical care research is the assessment of qualitative aspects of medical care. Clearly, nonmaterial variables are difficult to describe, let alone quantify (Kohn and White 1976), which is why subsequent research might benefit from Antonovsky's model (1979) of utilization and satisfaction. The model draws on the sociocultural environment such as the class differences between providers and patients as well as physicians' tolerance of ambiguity when patients describe symptoms. Physicians at Villa O'Higgins were young and from considerably higher-income backgrounds than their patients, and most expected to enter more lucrative private practice in the future. Despite the class disparity between physicians and patients at Villa O'Higgins, provider concern for patients played a considerable role in patients' help-seeking behavior and evaluation of care.

V
Spatial Organization and Medical Care Accessibility

Health care delivery systems are as diverse as the political, social, and economic milieux within which they operate (Roemer 1985; Kohn and White 1976). They can vary widely in their funding sources, their internal organizational structures, methods of payments, and physician-patient relationships (Joseph and Phillips 1984: 11–17). Harloe, for instance, has argued that comparing the range of diversity in various aspects of delivery systems in capitalist and socialist societies yields potentially as much information about urban development as about the provision of human services. These studies "ensure that national and international characteristics of urban development are not confused, but also . . . enable a conscious recognition to be made by researchers of the limitations that the very conditions which surround their activity impose on the context of their work, conditions which are likely to be highlighted and contrasted by circumstances elsewhere" (1981: 185).

Social, urban, and medical geographers have become increasingly interested in the influence of national medical care policy on the location of salutary facilities. Mohan and Woods (1985) reviewed the spatial allocation of medical resources in England under the conservative government of Prime Minister Margaret Thatcher by considering many factors that influence the spatial organization of health services such as historical patterns of service delivery, urban morphology, class struggle, and patterns of residential segregation. Clearly, the spatial distribution of public clinics or private physician surgeries cannot be examined as a virtual abstraction. No social public service can exist as an independent and static artifact, because it derives from dynamic social and political forces. Lefebvre has remarked that "space has been shaped and moulded from historical and natural elements, but this has been a political process. Space is political and ideological. It is a product literally filled with ideologies" (1978: 341).

This chapter attempts to trace the impact that Chile's medical care policies have had on the spatial organization of primary care clinics in Santiago by analyzing the distribution of the city's public and private primary medical care facilities. This pattern is then compared with patterns in Canada and the United States, which were selected for several reasons. Most researchers working only with English-language materials are likely to be familiar with the medical care systems of the United States and Canada (though the case of Great Britain is also well known). Furthermore, the emergence of a larger private medical market in Chile contrasts with Canada, where the private medical sector is small and most medical care is subsidized by the federal and provincial governments. It also contrasts with the United States, where private medical care predominates. Although there is a spate of research examining the relationship between national medical care policies in North America and the distribution of medical personnel, little research in this field has been carried out in Latin America.

Private physicians' locations in these three countries reflect compromises between patients' wishes to minimize travel distance and physicians' needs for nearby hospital and diagnostic facilities. The literature on the location of primary care facilities in the United States, and to a lesser extent Canada, provides a backdrop against which the Chilean case can be compared, showing to what extent the spatial organization of private physicians in Chile is the result of similar medical care policies and economic forces at work in North America.

An underlying assumption of this chapter, and indeed this book, is that medical care policy in Chile is a subsystem of a larger political and economic system. Accordingly, changes within the medical sector can be detected at the urban scale. The chapter also illustrates the differences between the two major research areas of medical geography: epidemiological geography (disease ecology), on the one hand, and the spatial organization (help-seeking behavior) of patients, on the other. Epidemiological geography examines the human-land vector relationship in the spread and prophylaxis of disease. It includes traditional disease studies that have been carried out since the time of Hippocrates and that have been reintroduced into medical research since the eighteenth century (Mayer 1982; Barret 1980). This perspective is well represented by the classic works of the French physician-geographer May (1950; 1958) and contributions by Weil and Kvale (1985), Meade (1980), Haggett (1976), Schiel and Wepfer (1976), and Hunter (1974). Spatial organization examines medical care planning and service delivery, the location of medical care facilities, and the help-seeking behavior of patients (Mayhew 1986; Joseph and Phillips 1984; Dever 1980; Pyle 1979: 165–267; Shannon and Dever 1974).

Three Geographic Approaches to Medical Care Organization

Three major lines of thought have been characterized within human geography that encompass the major paradigmatic and methodological approaches to the study of spatial behavior (Johnston 1977). These are the neoclassical, the humanistic, and the structuralist. Although these approaches are not mutually exclusive, they cover many of the philosophical and methodological perspectives of contemporary human geography.

NEOCLASSICAL/FUNCTIONAL APPROACH

The neoclassical/functional approach is based on models that treat the location of economic activities and access to them as a function of price. Studies of primary care suggest a trade-off in the search for care between the costs of travel (temporal, financial, and psychological) and the degree of specialty. According to classical locational theory, primary care providers would be expected to be less expensive, more abundant, and more dispersed than specialists. This pattern results because most primary services (internal and family medicine, pediatrics) are midorder economic activities, and specialty care (plastic and reparatory surgery, intensive care medicine, neurology) are higher-order economic activities.

Regardless of their specialties, private physicians tend to set up practices in the affluent neighborhoods where their clientele reside. In Santiago, for example, private physicians are concentrated in the highest-income neighborhoods in metropolitan Santiago, Providencia and Las Condes. The presence of few private physicians in low-income districts indicates the opposite: that most consumers lack the purchasing power or the need (given the availability of free SNSS clinics nearby) for frequent use of fee-for-service doctors. This relationship has become an axiom of economic geography and is generally substantiated in the free-market medical setting of the United States.

The application of Central Place Theory to physicians' services requires a few qualifiers. Points of access or entry to a medical market hierarchy are at the lowest echelon of the system (the doctor's office), but medical care consumers can not normally move through that hierarchy without physician referral. Unlike in most service industries, access to specialized and higher-order services in the medical industry tends to move vertically, with important gatekeepers at each stage: from general practitioner, to medical specialist, and finally to a hospital or other specialized treatment center.

Another caveat in using neoclassical or functional approaches is that they fail to relate the economic pattern of physician location back to the system of production or class relations. Rather, the distribution of physicians and patients is assumed to be a response to market forces and not personal tastes, such as the prestige that is tied to being located in an affluent neighborhood (Mayhew 1986). It is well established that the majority of U.S. physicians come from upper-income backgrounds and that they choose to locate in similar neighborhoods. In addition, physicians with rural upbringings are more likely to settle in rural areas (where physician coverage is most lacking). These patterns, derived from physicians' individual experiences and social class, are not well explained by the neoclassical or functional approach.

HUMANISTIC APPROACH

Humanistic or behavioral geographers challenge the neoclassical study of human spatial behavior. While neoclassicists argue that economic forces operate whether or not people recognize them as such, humanistic geographers contend that individuals experience the world in unique ways that defy verifiable normative laws like those found in the positivist branches of human geography (Tuan 1976; Buttimer 1976). The association of this branch of human geography with phenomenology implies that individual human experiences, not just market forces, influence spatial decision making (Sayer 1984). Except for the study by Arze (1984), the humanistic approach has not been used in studies of the locational patterns of primary care providers in Santiago.

A humanistic perspective on the location of primary facilities would not ignore the importance of price and distance between user and provider. It would, however, also consider the life experiences of individual practitioners in determining where they set up practice. Longnecker (1975) found that just over half (56 percent) of his twenty-two-state sample of family practice residents at rural facilities were raised in communities of less than 50 thousand inhabitants. Other research also suggests that physicians are likely to choose practice locations resembling the place of their upbringings (Fein 1956; Brown and Belcher 1966; Paul 1978). Thus nonpecuniary and individual preferences, not part of neoclassical economic perspectives, influence physician locations (Ernst and Yett 1985: 56–90).

STRUCTURALIST APPROACH

A recent addition to human geography is the institutional Marxist, or structuralist, approach as outlined by Harvey (1973) and Peet (1975). Although there are a number of interpretations of how Marxist inquiry should be conducted in the social sciences, common tenets exist. Verification and use of the scientific method is difficult, structuralists argue, because logical positivists fail to separate social problems (i.e., the unequal distribution of health or educational services) from their underlying causes. Patterns of inequity result from long-term and complex injustices that are founded in class and labor relations (de Vise 1973).

Structuralist geographers argue that the documentation of a social injustice is merely a symptom of a larger process of alienation that affects the poor. Positivist methods of analysis in human geography may be useless or irrelevant if one believes that "mapping even more evidence of man's patent inhumanity to man is counter-revolutionary in the sense that it allows the bleeding-heart liberal to pretend he is contributing to a solution when in fact he is not" (Harvey 1973: 27, cited in Smith 1974: 137).

Marxists contend that behavioralists and logical positivists ignore the realities of decision making in the marketplace and that humanists make light of socioeconomic restrictions placed on consumers and providers in the marketplace. Similarly, Marxist geographers criticize positivist approaches because they often explain individual, household, and aggregate behavior with little regard for such institutional parameters as class, gender, race, and ethnicity. A premise of this inquiry is that locational behavior is principally determined by power, predominantly economic power. If this is true, then geographers should consider the relevant political economy of a particular study by considering who benefits (and who does not) in the marketplace, as entrepreneurs search out new investment areas. Housing market studies in the United States (Harvey 1975) and Canada (Harris 1984) have been carried out in this vein.

Extending this line of thought to the Chilean case indicates that the government intervenes in medical care because marketplace imperfections make it impossible to satisfy all medical care needs. In Chile, private physicians are not willing to lower their fees for the poor, thereby forcing the SNSS to intervene. Most Chilean physicians work in the public sector while maintaining a small private practice. This pattern helps to ensure that the needs of the medically indigent are met and the incomes of physicians remain well above the national average. The SNSS, moreover, guarantees a minimum level of medical care for the cheap labor pool so that capitalism can continue. Excess value accrues to employers, who in turn pay taxes that finance the system (Kolakowski 1978). The cost paid by SNSS users is long waiting in difficult conditions (i.e., early morning queues outside clinics).

Nongeographers have contributed much to leftist critiques of modern medicine. Doyal and Pennell (1979) have argued that attributing all illnesses and maladies to capitalism in all places at all times yields little theoretical or political value. Among their many theses is the contention that national medical care systems seek to maintain a healthy—but not too healthy—labor force; fit workers might find it less easy to tolerate sedentary and boring jobs. A healthier labor force, they argue, might demand higher wages and more pleasing work settings, which would lower profits for employers (Doyal and Pennel 1979: 40). Castells (1978) has argued that many Western European countries provide a variety of social services out of, not benevolence, but fear that social unrest will ensue without them. This social unrest would spark revolutionary, or at least strong anticapitalist, movements. Illich (1975) has identified a social iatrogenisis in modern medical systems: an addiction of users to medical care as a solution to many of their problems, which in turn operates as a social control mechanism.

Marxist critiques of modern medicine contend that science is not valuefree and not ultimately beneficial to all. Rather, a myriad of value-ladden political, economic, and social forces shape the use of medical technology. Medical care in general is not always derived from a benevolent government or employer. Patterns of illness and health status vary by social class principally because profit determines the allocation of medical resources in capitalist economies. While the working classes in industrialized capitalist countries are generally less healthy than the rest of society, their efforts to procure comprehensive medical coverage through union demands are often thwarted if the private medical sector stands to make more money without such coverage. In Great Britain, for instance, the enactment of the National Health Service in 1948 has been interpreted by the left as a victory for the working class. But in the United States, there is compelling evidence that "the absence of a militant labour movement . . . must be seen as a major reason for the failure to develop an American state health system" (Doyal and Pennell 1979: 36). The American health system has perhaps been too potentially profitable to allow national health insurance to develop, and the demise of proposals for providing such insurance confirms that notion.

The Evolution of Urban Studies in Latin America

A major paradigmatic shift in Latin American urban research has occurred during the last two decades. Much of the early research assumed that economic development was a linear process that, in Rostowian terms, manifested a series of growth stages. The growth pole paradigm was an important cornerstone of this early thinking (Friedmann 1973). Since these stages were well documented in Europe and North America, it was expected that the Third World would replicate them if proper preconditions existed. This perspective of regional development, however, imposes rigid and mechanistic models of urban and regional growth and is unrealistic.

Mechanistic models of development such as the growth pole paradigm gradually fell into disfavor among Latinamericanists in the 1970s, who opted instead for studies that trace the internal changes of urban and national economies (Portes and Canak 1981). Rather than anticipating patterns of urban growth and economic development based on the historical experiences of industrial nations, they generated a new body of research that began to focus on the forces of urbanization and underdevelopment within a historical and international context. These studies have emphasized the adaptation of those poor who have not been absorbed by the formal industrial economy (Anthony 1979; Roberts 1978; Lomnitz 1978; Walton 1977; Perlman 1976; Collier 1976; McGee 1971; Vekemans et al. 1970; Hardoy 1969; and Quijano 1967). According to earlier studies of the 1960s, labor and capital should flow to labor- and capital-poor regions, thereby stimulating development. Despite massive intraregional migration and heavy borrowing of captial, Latin America had not developed to the extent anticipated by mechanistic models of development (Muñoz 1982).

Contemporary paradigms of Latin American urban research reject the notion that the failure of Latin American cities to replicate the economic development of industrial nations has resulted in the underdevelopment of the region. This research highlights both the uniqueness of the urban poor in certain spatial and historical contexts and the interrelatedness of national and regional economies in the world capitalist system. Since Latin American cities are in the process of adaptation to urban growth and a changing world economy, they do not necessarily conform to models based on North American and Western European experiences.

Urban geographers have analyzed how the morphology and growth of Latin American cities differ from their North American counterparts. The morphological model of Griffin and Ford

(1980), for example, shows that a small middle-income group and a curtailed highway network have limited massive suburbanization on the scale found in North America. This model also notes that the industrial zone that surrounds the Central Business district (CBD) of a Latin American city takes advantage of the cheap labor of inner-city residents. Ford and Griffin depict the Latin American city as ruled by a single transport artery that runs from the CBD outward. Unlike in North American cities, the bulk of the poor in Latin American cities are concentrated at the urban fringe. Elbow (1983) applied this model to secondary cities in Guatemala and found that the Griffin and Ford model fits well. Still other models of the Latin American city emphasize how the colonial structure in city design has been retained by shifting high-density residential development away from the colonial core (Bähr and Mertins 1982; Bähr and Riesco 1981; Ingram and Carroll 1981).

Latin American urban research has also addressed the rapid post-World War II population growth, which has often been in excess of 4 percent per year. Specifically, this research has considered rural-urban migration streams and the various stages that this process entails (Brown and Lawson 1985; Thomas and Hunter 1980; Turner 1968; Mangin 1967). These studies conclude that rapid urban growth and urbanization have altered the location of traditional economic activities; land use and housing regulations have not kept pace with burgeoning population growth (López 1981; Trivelli 1981; Bähr and Riesco 1981; Bähr 1978). Shantytowns are mute evidence of the void between population growth and adequate housing.

The Social Ecology of Greater Santiago

LOCATION AND SETTLEMENT

Santiago de Chile is located in one of a series of valleys in central Chile. The colonial core of the city is laid out in the traditional gridiron pattern that typifies most Latin American cities and towns (Stanislawski 1946; 1947). City blocks surrounding the Plaza de Armas, the main town square, have changed little since the town was designed in the sixteenth century under the guidelines of the Law of the Indies. This colonial section of Santiago lies at the foot of a small hill in the city center, Santa Lucia, an eroded remnant of the larger San Cristobal Hills. Originally, two branches of the Mapocho river flanked the city plaza to the north and south, but the latter was filled in the last century to facilitate travel to the center of town. At present, the main thoroughfare, the Alameda, covers this former southern branch of the Mapocho river.

Santiago is a distinctively sectoral city (figure 12). Major transport arteries extend from the old colonial center in spoke-like fashion. Settlement has been contained in the north and east, where a series of small hills and the Andes cordillera lie, respectively. At the southern edge of the metropolis, the valley floor widens and serves as the urban fringe of the metropolitan area, where farmland is being replaced by legal and squatter settlement.

Santiago has a conspicuously low skyline for a city of 4.5 million inhabitants. A few skyscrapers tower over the city center, but only in the last three decades have modern high-rise apartments been feasible, with the advent of seismic-resistant construction. (Historically, the nation has been plagued with considerable seismic activity.) Santiago's relative low density and grey concrete-veneer buildings give it an appearance similar to early-twentieth-century Moscow and Paris (Fuller 1972).

The social ecology of the city changed little until new suburbs opened up for the elite in the early part of this century. An increasingly congested city center, the growth of retail trade, and a general loss of amenities around the colonial core attracted many elite to new suburbs in the northeast in the 1920s and 1930s. This section of the city, the *barrio alto* in the municipalities of Providencia and Las Condes, offered a more country-like residence where French- and English-style homes could stand on large lots that were unavailable in the colonial

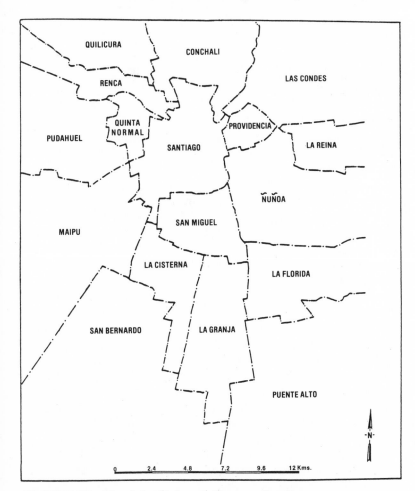

FIGURE 12. Municipalities of Greater Santiago

core. While upper-incomes residents took advantage of these suburbs, middle-income groups tended to move to the city center in succession (Bähr and Riesco 1981; Bähr and Mertins 1982; Amato 1970).

RESIDENTIAL SEGREGATION

One facet of the contemporary social ecology of Greater Santiago is its level of income segregation (figure 13). Conventional methods for assessing such segregation in North America often use city directories to document home ownership and tenancy rates. In North America, the working class (i.e., low-income residents) exhibit higher tenancy rates than middle- and upper-income groups (Harris 1984; Saunders 1979). Although such directories are not widely available in Latin America, their use would reveal a different pattern from the North American: both the rich and poor have high levels of ownership, while middle-income groups show high tenancy rates (Gilbert and Ward 1978; Roberts 1978). The wealthy mortgage homes through conventional lending institutions and the poor construct dwellings from discarded or low-cost materials in slums, referred to in various parts of Latin America as *barriadas, callampas, poblaciones, pueblos jovenes, ranchos, villas miserias,* and *favelas.* Although squatters initially occupy lands illegally, they frequently assume legal ownership over time (Roberts 1978; Collier 1976).

A recent study (Scarpaci et al. 1987) assessed the degree of segregation in Greater Santiago using data from a 1977 transportation study. Household income data were used to examine segregation patterns in 202 zones and 1,800 households (UCFI 1977). A matrix of income quintiles for each neighborhood was constructed. The variance of each quintile was derived by the percentage of households that fell into each quintile (about 40 households per group). The level of income segregation was defined by the number of standard deviations beyond the mean of each quintile. Neighborhoods with "very high" segregation lie 3 or more standard deviations beyond the mean; "high" segregation falls between 1.01 and 2.99 standard deviations; and "low" segregation reflects a value of less than 1 standard deviation.

Figure 13 shows a high degree of residential segregation in the

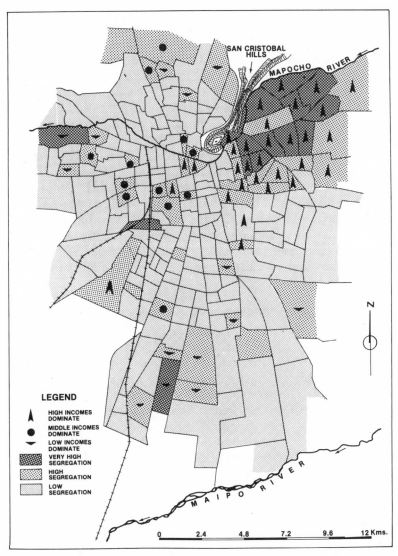

FIGURE 13. Income Segregation in Greater Santiago, 1977

upper-income districts of Las Condes and Providencia. South of this highly segregated high-income area lie the middle-income municipalities of Ñuñoa and La Reina, where income and occupational structures are similar to those of the municipality of Santiago. In general, municipalities in the south (La Florida, San Miguel, La Granja, La Cisterna) and west (Pudahuel, Renca) house low-income groups in highly segregated neighborhoods. Social distance in the metropolis is heightened by the San Cristobal Hills, which separate low-income Conchali from the wealthy northeast. Thus topographic barriers to the north and east (the Andes mountains), coupled with a middle-income district to the south, afford *barrio alto* residents a broad buffer zone between themselves and the poor. Income levels drop off in all directions with increasing distance from the *barrio alto*. Few Latin American cities have high-income districts like Providencia and La Condes that enjoy such isolation from the visual blight of poor neighborhoods.

ORGANIZATION OF PRIMARY MEDICAL CARE

As the economy has worsened and as employer-sponsored medical programs have become more expensive, primary medical care systems in Santiago have changed. One emerging trend is the SNSS clinics have become more important to *obreros* and the poor. The sixty-four SNSS primary care clinics *(consultorios periféricos)* in Greater Santiago form the largest primary care network in the public or private sector. These clinics are the main entry point into the public medical care network, delivering about 70 percent of all primary care in the metropolis and servicing an average of 47 thousand patients per clinic (Ministerio de Salud 1983). This mean figure, however, does not reflect the wide range of service delivery, given that some clinics deliver care to as many as 100 thousand Santiaguinos (personal communications, Dr. Max Monteros, 1984).[1] Referrals made at the clinics are directed to a major hospital for secondary and tertiary care.

SITING OF SNSS CLINICS

Procedures for locating SNSS clinics in Greater Santiago do not draw on methods of locational analysis nor are they derived from electoral demands. While the public has not been able to request social services through elected representatives since 1973, Ministry of Health officials still claim that citizens influence the siting of health clinics. According to the Secretary of the Metropolitan Health Service, three kinds of demand exist for locating new SNSS facilities.

The first is spontaneous demand (so named because of its sudden and ad hoc nature), whereby the SNSS satisfies the demands of population growth by establishing a new facility in a particular part of a city. Information about latent demand comes to the attention of the government from clinic personnel who notice that a disproportionate number of patients come from areas beyond a clinic's designated service area. Much spontaneous demand results from high population growth at the urban fringe in the southern and western districts of the metropolis. Topographic barriers are absent in these districts, and they are the only regions where major new settlement is taking place. In September and October of 1983, for example, southern Santiago was the site of large-scale land invasions by several thousand squatters. This land invasion *(toma)* placed a heavy burden on nearby clinics.[2]

A second method of siting clinics results from public demand expressed through neighborhood organizations called *juntas de vecinos*. These voluntary organizations allegedly represent the needs of local residents in requesting police and fire protection, primary and secondary education, sewage and public works projects, and medical care. Little research has focused on the *juntas de vecinos*, which are, essentially, the only collective decision making groups of citizens in authoritarian Chile. Ostensibly, neighborhood residents can request an SNSS clinic through their municipal government, which in turn passes the request on to the National Planning Office and the Ministry of Health. The efficacy of these *juntas de vecinos* is suspect, given that decision making is secretive at high levels of government (Scarpaci et al. 1988).

A third manner by which SNSS clinics are located is through mayoral appeal—requests by municipal (county) mayors *(alcaldes)* for medical services for their jurisdictions. These officials are not elected to office; rather, they are assigned by President Pinochet or by the regional military governor *(intendente)*. Although the population en masse is a factor in siting health clinics, individual consumers are the least influential agents in the public medical system in contemporary authoritarian Chile.

SNSS CLINIC DISTRIBUTION

A cursory examination of the distribution of SNSS clinics indicates a fairly uniform pattern throughout Greater Santiago, although clinics are almost absent from the core of the *barrio alto* (figure 14). Low-income areas in the west, north, and south appear to be well covered. Figure 14 is derived from a proximal map that estimates the service area of each clinic based on distance, as opposed to artificial administrative boundaries, which users often ignore. A proximal map displays the clinic service area by assigning to every location the data value associated with the nearest public health clinic (Dougenik and Sheehan 1979). The map is comprised of six separate computer-generated maps of the six health districts in the metropolitan region. The closest clinic to any given point (a potential household of clinic users) within a health district can be determined from this map. Though the distribution of clinics appears to be quite uniform, service areas in the southeastern region are larger than elsewhere. Accordingly, residents within this health district travel farther for care. The western portions of the metropolis have the smallest service areas, affording low-income residents there greater spatial access than other SNSS users.

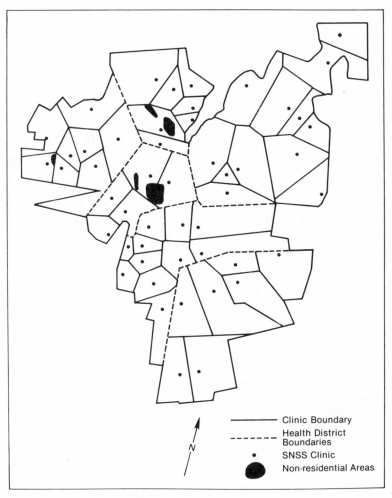

Clinic Boundary
Health District
Boundaries
SNSS Clinic
Non-residential Areas

N

FIGURE 14. SNSS Clinics in Greater Santiago, 1983

NEAREST-NEIGHBOR INDEX

The nearest neighbor index was used to examine whether the 1983 pattern of SNSS clinics in Santiago was random. Since low-income neighborhoods are not randomly distributed throughout the city, it was expected that the clinics that serve them were also located in a nonrandom fashion.[3] To ensure the proper measurement of the nearest-neighbor index, smaller satellite municipalities of the metropolis (San Bernardo, Puente Alto, Maipu, Quilicura) were excluded. The boundary area was drawn well within the outermost limits of the metropolitan area, excluding ten of the sixty-four SNSS clinics in the region.[4]

Following Hammond and McCullagh (1974), two hypotheses were established:

| Null hypothesis | The distributional pattern of SNSS clinics in Greater Santiago is similar to a pattern produced by the independent random location of each point. |
| Alternative hypothesis | The distributional pattern of SNSS clinics in Greater Santiago is not random. |

Nearest-neighbor or order-neighbor analysis calculates an index measure of R with theoretical values ranging from 0 (indicating perfectly clustered points) to 2.149 (denoting a uniform distribution pattern). A perfectly dispersed pattern would exhibit the form of a triangular lattice (Silk 1979: 109). The measure is calculated by dividing the mean distance between nearest neighbor points in an area by the mean distance expected from an equal number of points distributed randomly in the same area. First-order analysis assesses local conditions by measuring point-pattern distributions based on the nearest point (clinic) to each point. Second-order analysis assesses regional conditions by measuring point-pattern distributions based on the second-nearest point (clinic) to each point.[5]

Calculations executed by a BASIC program (Buckner 1985) for

both first- and second-order (neighbor) points reveal a nonrandom pattern. First-order results generated an R-value of 0.776, indicating a cluster pattern. Second-order results yielded an R-value of 1.251, representing a distribution of clinics that tends toward uniformity. In other words, the point-pattern distributions of SNSS clinics throughout Greater Santiago are not randomly distributed. First- and second-order results show that clinics are regionally dispersed and tend to cluster locally. This test corroborates the qualitative appraisal that clinics are concentrated in poorer parts of the metropolis, where SNSS users reside.

ACCESSIBILITY OF SNSS CLINICS

Gravity, location-allocation, and linear-programming models are useful in evaluating the accessibility of public services (Haynes and Fotheringham 1984; Scarpaci 1984b; Swain 1981). In the United States, for instance, a number of these models have been used in studying locational aspects of public health clinics (Calvo and Marks 1973; Earickson 1970; Morrill et al. 1970). In general, these methods have addressed the spatial behavior of patients in free-market medical systems as well as the locational efficiency of these delivery systems. These methods are useful in addressing questions of equity of medical care services and access to primary care (Kirby 1983; 1982; Hodge and Gattrell 1976; Monroe and McGrew 1974; Morrill 1984; Symons 1971).

A modified version of the gravity model (Harris 1954) is especially relevant to the present study because it includes a distance-decay parameter (or function) and measures the potential accessibility or attractiveness of clinics.[6] The nodal accessibility of SNSS clinics is measured by a simple index derived from the gravity model. Two mapping exercises of accessibility were used in this study. Each exercise generated potential accessibility surfaces of fifty-four SNSS clinics based on measurements from 394 control points. These control points were derived by taking a systematic sampling at regular intervals from a grid superimposed over the city. Only control points falling within the contiguous metropolitan areas were used to map accessibility surfaces. Each clinic was weighted by the number of physician hours supplied there (Knox 1979; Smith 1979; Symons 1971). The computation is derived as follows:

$$Ai = \sum_{i=1}^{n=54} \left(\frac{Sj}{Dij^k}\right),$$

Where

Ai = summary index of accessibility of clinics at point i,
Sj = size of the clinic measured by the number of physician hours worked weekly,
Dij = distance between i and j,
k = distance-decay function denoting the fall-off in attendance to a given facility,
n = number of clinics.

The accessibility surface reveals considerable disparity among clinic service areas (figure 15). Southern municipalities in the metropolitan area (La Florida, La Granja, La Cisterna) have less-accessible clinics than most of the metropolis. In contrast, the large low-income districts in the western metropolitan area (Pudahuel, Renca) fare relatively well and could be interpreted as relatively "overdoctored." No bias is seen in the middle- and upper-income municipalities of Providencia, Las Condes, La Reina, and Ñuñoa; their potential accessibility is average. This measure of the accessibility of primary care, therefore, representing one indicator of the geography of well-being (Knox 1980) in Greater Santiago, indicates both relative cases of overdoctored and underdoctored areas, but not at the expense of either poor or wealthy districts.

The specification of the distance-decay parameter *(k)* is significant because different accessibility surfaces can be pro-

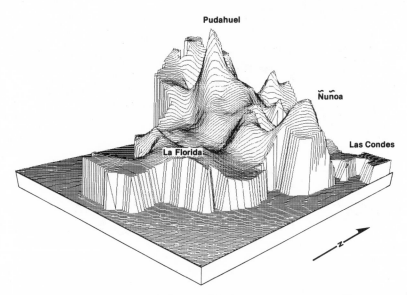

FIGURE 15. Accessibility Surfaces Among SNSS Clinics

duced as the value of k changes. The rationale behind the careful specification of distance-decay parameters is illustrated by the following example. If a particular point were equidistant from two points, say clinics A and B, and clinic B offered more hours of medical care, then one would expect potential interaction to be greater at the larger facility (Fotheringham 1979: 197). The resultant accessibility value will vary with distance-decay parameter k. A small value of k (0.5) emphasizes general effects of clinic proximity while a large value of k (3.0) highlights local effects of a clinic's relative location.[7]

Figure 16 reveals the changes in the accessibility surfaces when k = 0.5, 1.0, 1.5, 2.0, 2.5, and 3.0. The local effects caused by the larger distance-decay parameters produce a more differentiated surface than smaller parameters. Large parameters highlight the local effects of two or more clinics located close to each other. As illustrated by figure 15, the western

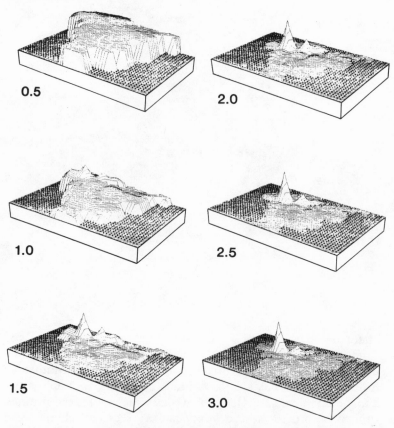

FIGURE 16. Accessibility Surfaces Among SNSS Clinics, Six
Distance-Decay Parameters

areas show the highest indexes of accessibility to SNSS clinics. This finding points out the need to increase the number of physician hours or facilities in the low-income municipalities of La Cisterna, La Granja, and La Florida if their care is to be commensurate with other low-income districts.

The proximal map, nearest-neighbor analysis, and accessibility surface reveal common features. Southern portions of the metropolis have larger service areas and are underserved with respect to other indigent areas. Maps of nodal accessibility (figure 15 and 16) consistently revealed "valleys" in the south. In contrast, the clinics in the western municipality of Pudahuel have the smallest service areas as well as the highest "peaks." The western and, to a lesser extent, the central municipalities (Ñuñoa, San Miguel, and Santiago) offer greater potential accessibility because of the number of physician hours provided and their smaller service areas. The main policy recommendation is that access to SNSS clinics in the southern part of the metropolis be enhanced either by establishing new facilities or, the less-expensive option, by increasing physician hours at target facilities.

DISTRIBUTION OF THE FONASA PHYSICIANS

The spatial distribution of any professional group such as physicians, lawyers, and accountants provides insight into the social ecology of the city. In the free marketplace, professionals select office locations in response to factors that are shaped by the forces of competition, and are oriented toward user demand.

Two data sources exist with regard to the location of doctors' offices in the FONASA program. One source covers 1978, the last year of operation for the SERMENA, the predecessor to the FONASA system. At that time, the SERMENA was divided into two levels of care, rather than FONASA's three. While these levels of care carry different costs (level one is the least expensive), the clinical competence of providers is the same. Amenities such as the comfort of the waiting room and waiting time vary. As of 1983, however, the list of the FONASA physicians had merely been updated by including new physicians who entered the FONASA or by registering former SERMENA physicians who changed their affiliation from one level of care to another. Figures 17 and 18 show, respectively, the distribution of SERMENA (1978) and FONASA (1983). Together, the maps provide a reasonable representation of the

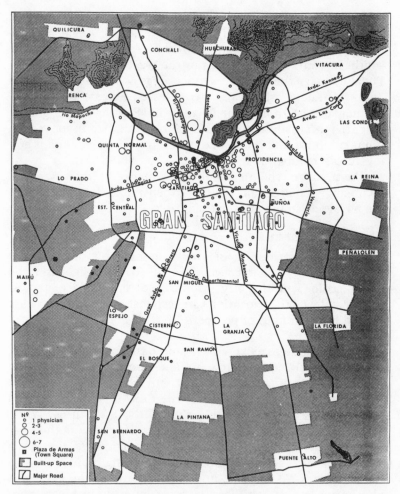

FIGURE 17. Distribution of SERMENA Physicians, 1978

distribution of physicians affiliated with the FONASA in 1983 (personal communication, Ernesto Miranda, FONASA, October 1983).

The FONASA physicians were generally located in the cen-

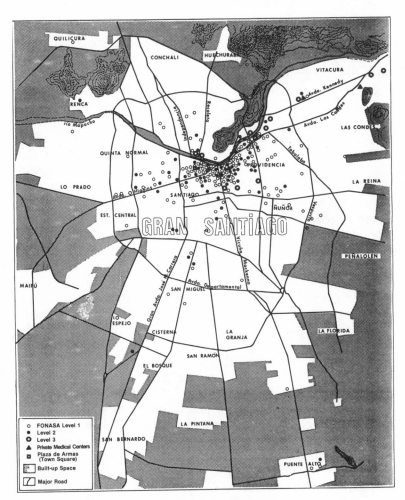

FIGURE 18. Distribution of FONASA Physicians, 1983.

ter of Santiago, with three distinct clusters near main roads and downtown hospitals. One concentration is between the Catholic University and Salvador Hospital. Another cluster can be seen along the main thoroughfare, the Alameda, which runs westward above the subway system of Santiago, the *Metro*. A third grouping is somewhat less dense: lying north of the central business district along Independencia and Recoleta avenues. Several major hospitals are in this part of the city, including the large teaching hospital at the medical school of the University of Chile.

In short, the FONASA physicians are clustered in the city center, close to large hospitals and many public and private white-collar workers, who have patronized them since the 1930s under the SERMENA. Unlike the pattern in SNSS clinics, offices of FONASA general practitioners are not dispersed throughout the residential areas of their patients. Rather, their locations maximize access to hospitals and the workplaces of their patients.

Two types of FONASA specialists, plastic surgeons and doctors of critical care medicine, were selected to determine whether different distributions exist between the FONASA specialists and physicians in general.[8] It was expected that these specialists' practices would be located between hospitals where they held staff privileges and the high-income neighborhoods where they or their patients reside. Both figures 19 and 20 substantiate this expectation.

The two specialist groups are concentrated in the *barrio alto*, clustering between the major hospitals in the downtown area (where the FONASA general practitioners are clustered) and the residences of their high-income clientele. Their "uptown" location is reached via the main thoroughfare of Providencia Avenue, a continuation of the Alameda. Providencia Avenue is over the *Metro*, thus providing patients convenient access to specialists' offices by automobile or rail. The location of this sample of FONASA specialists in pleasant high-income neighborhoods in the Santiago suburbs is similar to the pattern observed by Rosenburg (1979) in his study of physicians in Toronto, granting more grounds to the comparison between Chile and Canada, which follows in a later section.

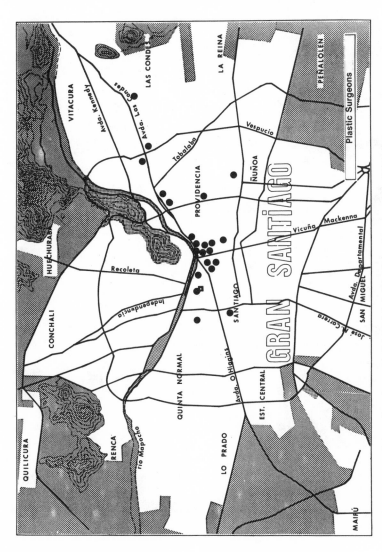

FIGURE 19. *Distribution of FONASA Plastic Surgeons, 1983*

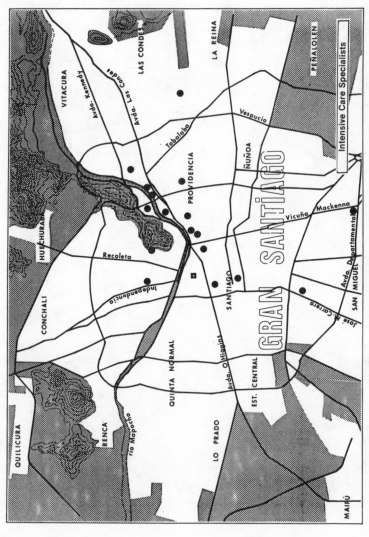

FIGURE 20. *Distribution of FONASA Intensive Care Specialists, 1983*

DISTRIBUTION OF GROUP PRIVATE MEDICAL PRACTICES

Many practitioners in the private medical sector have arrangements *(convenios)* with the FONASA, ISAPRE, and other medical programs. Because of the recent creation of these programs (early 1980s), the description of the distribution of private physicians will serve as a "snapshot" of the early stage of a boom, a bust, or the stabilization of the private medical market in Chile under the restructured medical system.

One feature common in both U.S. and Chilean private medical group practices is the provision of a wide array of in-house services, ranging from general practitioners and specialists to a variety of laboratory procedures. Evidence from the United States suggests that private medical centers can generate economies of scale (particularly with lab services) that ultimately result in lower real costs. In addition, they depend less on outside laboratories or specialists (Roemer and Schonick 1973).

The potential savings generated by group practices, however, has not always been passed on to consumers. A number of researchers have argued that there is an easy and tempting opportunity to request excessive and duplicative services (Kirkham 1977; Baehr 1966). While many of these potentially excessive services are in response to the threat of malpractice litigation, they generate additional income for practitioners who are partial owners of the clinic or who participate in profit sharing. This is not, however, the usual case with HMOs, since there is little or no fee-for-service care.

Studies related to the distribution of medical centers in Santiago are fairly new, receiving impetus from the free-market changes initiated by the Pinochet regime. A pioneer study by Jiménez de la Jara (1982b) documented the growth of physicians' advertising in the Greater Santiago telephone directory between 1975 and 1982. The number of medical centers, many of which are actually small private hospitals, grew by 145 percent in this period. This growth was concentrated in the upper-income neighborhoods of Las Condes and Providencia. Jiménez de la Jara also compared the financial "survival rate" of private ambulatory care and in-patient facilities. He concluded that "the strictly private hospital, operating as a normal private enterprise, has costs that surpass its revenues and that quickly place the firm in economic insolvency. . . . The private health care firm that works with diagnosis and ambulatory care has, conversely, a quick return on its initial investment and generates easy capital for its owners, who are usually physicians" (1982b: 187; my translation).

The rank order of the municipalities containing private medical clinics was correlated with both the rank order of the average 1983 family monthly incomes, and the municipal income (mean income multiplied by municipal population) of the municipalities where the private clinics are located (table 19).[9] It was assumed that there would be a strong and positive re-

TABLE 19
Private Medical Clinics and Income of Population, Seven
Greater Santiago Municipalities, 1983

Municipality	Private Medical Clinics	Ratio of Private Clinics, Greater Santiago: Municipality	Per Person Monthly Income	Population (Thousands)	Municipal Income (Billions)
Santiago	150	1.0	10,411	619.1	6.4
Providencia	87	4.1	25,006	114.8	2.9
Ñuñoa	25	14.5	8,681	421.9	3.7
Las Condes	21	17.2	18,681	262.9	4.9
San Miguel	13	27.7	4,352	359.0	1.6
La Florida	9	40.0	7,287	191.3	1.4
La Cisterna	9	40.0	5,170	360.1	4.9

Sources: SNSS, March 1983; Department of Economics and Administration, University of Chile; INE 1982, p. 20.
Note: Income based on mid-year value of Chilean peso. Population and income data do not include municipalities established in 1984.

lationship between the presence of private medical centers and both family monthly income and total municipal income. This relationship was confirmed by a Spearman coefficient of $r_s = .732$ $(p = .05)$ for both income measures.

DISTRIBUTION OF SOLO PRIVATE MEDICAL PRACTICES

A study by Arze (1984) analyzed changes in the location of solo medical practices from 1950 to 1980 and the reasons for physicians' selecting office locations in 1982 (using a 50 percent systematic sample of the 1950 and 1980 physician listings in the Santiago telephone directory). During the thirty years, practices seem to have dispersed from the city center toward the east and northeast (figures 21, 22). In 1950, 83 percent of all physicians were located in the municipality of Santiago, with only 10 percent in the municipality of Providencia. By 1980, this proportion of physicians shifted to 40 percent and 28 percent, respectively (Arze 1984: 197). Although physicians had changed location, Arze was not able to conclude whether they had dispersed more than the general population.

A test was set up to determine whether physicians were changing their office locations from the city center to the suburbs at the same rate as the dispersion of the metropolitan population. The coefficient of localization was used to measure the concentration of private physicians. The measure examines the distribution of a particular phenomenon across a region relative to a base magnitude:

$$\mathrm{CL} = .5 \sum_i \left[\frac{M_i}{\sum\limits_i M_i} - \frac{P_i}{\sum\limits_i P_i} \right],$$

Where

CL = the coefficient of localization for private physicians in Greater Santiago,

M_i = the number of private medical doctors with an office in area i, and

P_i = the population of area i.

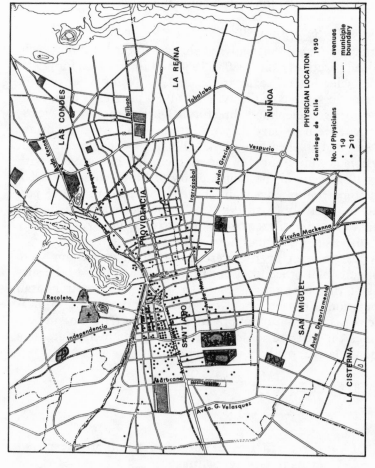

FIGURE 21. *Private Physician Locations, 1950*

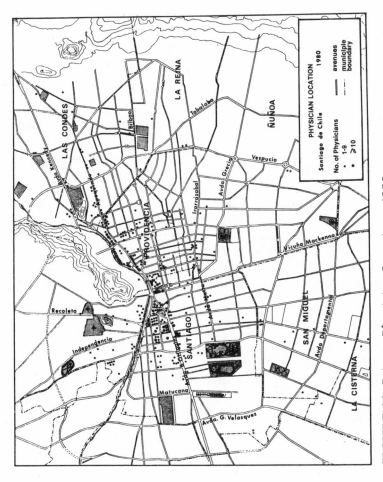

FIGURE 22. Private Physician Locations, 1980

Coefficient values range from 0 to 1. A value of 0 indicates that physicians are distributed throughout an area in exactly the same proportion as the general population. A value of 1 would occur only if physicians and the population were located in mutually exclusive areas (Joseph and Hall 1985: 152; Joseph and Bantock 1982; Joseph 1981; Joseph and Phillips 1984: 98; Lloyd and Dicken 1968).[10] Coefficients of localization were calculated using Arze's physician data.

The localization coefficients generated for 1950 and 1980 were .257 and .436 respectively (table 20). Unlike physicians in the United States, physicians in Santiago have become more spatially concentrated since World War II. The coefficient of localization test suggests that in 1980 private physicians who advertise in the telephone directory were 70 percent (.436/.257) more concentrated than in 1950. This strong concentration of physicians is similar to Rosenberg's (1983b) study of Toronto between 1951 and 1971. Given the patterns of physician concentration in Canada, Chile, and the United States, it appears that forces of the private medical marketplace act as a greater agent of dispersion than those of the more socialized medical systems of Canada and Chile.

TABLE 20
Physicians and Population, Five Greater Santiago Municipalities, 1950s and 1980s, and their Coefficients of Localization

Municipality	1950 Physicians	1952 Population	1980 Physicians	1982 Population
Santiago	347	515,800	194	619,105
Providencia	44	54,459	158	114,105
Las Condes	1	27,056	28	262,919
Ñuñoa	18	91,303	25	421,870
San Miguel	1	99,799	10	359,030
Total	411	788,417	415	1,777,694
Coefficient of localization	.257			.436

Arze (1984) interviewed twenty-two private physicians with solo practices in Santiago regarding the selection of their office sites. Physicians ranked locational attributes in order of importance as follows: proximity to the subway, closeness to support facilities (laboratories), good (nonrail) public transportation, an absence of noise, and proximity to major transport arteries. This ranking indicates that attributes important to both the practitioner (quiet places) and the consumer (good transportation) determine the location of private practitioners in Santiago. Although Arze's sample was small, the attributes of private-practice locations in Santiago are similar to the North American pattern, whose health policies are reviewed in the following section.

Health Policies and Physician Location in Canada and the United States

CANADA

Roemer (1977b) classified the Canadian medical system as a mixture of the traditional welfare state, where the national government ensures universal medical coverage regardless of income, and the socialist state, where private medical practice is quite small. Following the experience of Saskatchewan in the 1950s, other Canadian provinces voted in the 1960s to pay for medical care with public funds. Initially, provincial governments paid one-half the costs of all medical care, while the national government paid the other half. The purpose of this financial arrangement was twofold: (1) to slow down the rise in medical costs and (2) to provide service to the medically indigent.[11] Currently, medical care funds are allocated by block grants, and provincial governments manage these funds under broad national guidelines. In Ontario, for example, the provincial government pays 90 percent of the costs of medical care, while the consumer pays the rest. The proportion of funds paid by other provincial governments varies (Rosenberg 1983b).

Most studies on the location and distribution of physicians

128 § PRIMARY MEDICAL CARE IN CHILE

in Canada have been at the regional level (Thrall and Tsitandidis 1983; Roos et al. 1976; Spaulding and Spitzer 1972). This
literature has examined the significance of patient origins,
costs of travel to medical care, and the location and growth of
physician services. Bottomley (1971), however, pioneered work
on the intraurban spatial behavior of Canadian physicians. He
asked twenty general practitioners and twenty specialists to
rank seven criteria that might affect the attractiveness of doctors' offices. On the one hand, general practitioners, who depend very little on hospital equipment and services, claimed
that residing within five minutes of a hospital was the least
important attribute of their locations; they saw access to public transportation as the most important spatial attribute. On
the other hand, specialists said that access to public transportation was the least important factor, whereas proximity to hospitals was the most important. Bottomley's research shows the
significance of nonpecuniary factors, such as neighborhood
characteristics, when the price of medical care varies little.
Even when competition among physicians is not a function of
price, nonpecuniary factors still influence the location of physician practices.

Other studies on the location of physicians' offices in Canada have described the pattern of generalists versus specialists.
Spoerel (1974) determined that specialists in Ontario typically
located their practices in urban centers between two major
hospitals where they had staff privileges. General practitioners, however, were more evenly distributed throughout the
metropolitan area. Rosenburg (1979) concluded that physicians
in Toronto tended to concentrate in high-income neighborhoods with wide avenues, low crime rates, and little traffic
congestion, particularly if these neighborhoods were close to
major hospitals. Rosenburg compared the distribution of physicians in Toronto between 1951 and 1971 with the suburbanization of the metropolitan region. His nearest-neighbor analysis
showed that physician practices became less clustered between 1951 and 1971, and the number of locations decreased

(with more multiphysician practices per location) while the number of physicians increased. The twenty-year trend was characterized as a decline in the proportion of solo practices, as physicians opted for group practices in more aesthetically pleasing neighborhoods.[12]

UNITED STATES

Schultz (1969) was one of the first researchers to outline the expected points of access to primary medical care within an optimum central-place hierarchy of medical care services. He concluded that physicians' locations could not be characterized by the dictums of Central Place Theory, even when the assumptions of price and physician supply were relaxed. A number of factors account for the deviation from this theoretical pattern. American physicians operate as oligarchs, which distorts this geometric ideal. Physicians in the United States use the American Medical Association (which represents about half of all physicians) to (1) control the legal environment in which they work, (2) influence admissions criteria for medical schools, and (3) determine licensure criteria for their peers and auxiliary personnel. Further, Medicaid, Medicare and private insurance carriers have established price guidelines that distort free-market competition.

In 1983, Medicare shifted to a prospective payment system, with different charges in nine regions of the United States. These charges are based on 467 diagnostic-related groups (DRGs). If hospitals deliver care at costs less than that stipulated by the DRG, they keep the difference as a saving. If costs exceed the DRG, the hospital incurs the loss. These DRGs are the latest government plan to hold down health care costs (*Medical World News* 1985). These factors help explain why pure competition does not exist in the American medical market and why the locational patterns of physicians vary from central place theory.

State intervention in the U.S. medical market increased in the post-World War II period as evidenced by the Hill-Burton

Act (1946) and the creation of Medicaid and Medicare (1965). These programs attempted to increase hospital coverage in rural areas (Hill-Burton), and to reduce financial costs for the poor (Medicaid) and the elderly (Medicare). In a parallel trend, there was also a plethora of evaluation research on these programs. Hill-Burton funds did increase the number of hospitals in rural America, but the Medicaid and Medicare legislation has produced more questionable results. Yet, despite government and private insurance intervention in the U.S. medical marketplace, the United States still remains the largest private medical market in the world (Roemer 1977b). Although Medicaid sought to provide basic medical services for the poor, physicians clearly did not rush to set up medical practices in inner-city areas (Cugliani 1978). Somewhat unexpectedly, the urban poor have been treated in increasing numbers in the outpatient clinics and emergency rooms of large public hospitals. These facilities have become the "doctors' offices" of the urban poor of America—an outcome not anticipated by the writers of the 1965 legislation.

Luben et al. (1966) and Schneider (1967), whose foci are tied to the distance-decay paradigm in explaining the location of physicians, argued that specialists in the United States seek to minimize distance between the hospital and their private practices. General practitioners, however, wish to minimize distance between their homes and their practices if they do not have hospital duties. In contrast to the distance-decay paradigm, de Vise (1971; 1973) posited an ideological explanation of physician location, contending that physician ideology impedes the establishment of medical practices in underserved areas where the poor and minority groups reside. Physicians seek to maximize their lifetime incomes and recuperate as fast as possible opportunity costs incurred during their medical training. While attempts by the government to establish financing schemes such as Medicaid, Medicare, and Hill-Burton did not substantially alter physician behavior in the 1960s (Derbyshire 1969; Rayack 1964), there is some evidence that

HMOs are forcing physicians to be more price conscious (Homer 1982).

Shannon et al. (1978) reviewed the locational patterns of physicians in Washington, D.C., a city where blacks are the majority, to determine whether de Vise's (1971; 1973) assessment of physician location was valid. They found that low-income blacks overwhelmingly sought primary medical care in the emergency rooms and out-patient clinics of large hospitals. Somewhat unexpected, however, was the finding that about one-third of middle-income blacks also used hospital facilities for primary medical care, even though they could afford private practitioners. Blacks felt more comfortable when attended in the company of other blacks, regardless of their income level. In other words, less waiting time for private physicians was less important than being treated in settings with other blacks. On the supply side of primary medical care, this same study noted that 25 percent of private general practitioners in Washington, D.C., were concentrated within one mile of three major hospitals—a cluster pattern for a North American city.

Shannon and Dever (1974) noted the migration of physicians to the Sunbelt, particularly high-income metropolitan areas with large research and teaching hospitals (e.g., Atlanta, Houston, Chapel Hill, Miami). Rosenthal (1978) considered the locational pattern of physicians in the Miami, Fort Lauderdale, and West Palm Beach Standard Metropolitan Statistical Areas (SMSAs) between 1950 and 1970. He concluded that not only was there a strong and positive correlation between physician location in Sunbelt SMSAs but that high-income and high-density population areas were the strongest attractors of physician practices.

Dewey (1973) was one of the first researchers to describe primary medical care as a retail trade activity by documenting the increase of physicians' offices in shopping centers, large shopping malls, and midsize commerical centers. These sites provide consumers with the same access to primary care as to other retail activities. In the same analysis, Dewey confirmed the pattern observed by Morrill et al. (1970)—that physicians in the post-World War II period had gradually abandoned inner-city locations adjacent to hospitals (and that were undergoing ethnic and socioeconomic change) and had established practices in the affluent suburbs. Busch and Dale (1978) confirmed this trend, noting that the U.S. physician sets up practice in prosperous communities with support facilities.

Summing up, the following points highlight the North American pattern of physician location: (1) physicians have been gradually leaving city centers; (2) physicians are increasingly locating in affluent suburban neighborhoods; (3) specialists prefer to locate near large teaching hospitals; and (4) shopping centers and shopping malls increasingly house more physicians, emphasizing that primary medical care is a low- to mid-order service that is accessible by automobile travel.

Discussion and Summary

This chapter has examined the role that the type of medical care financing plays in influencing the location of public clinics and private physicians. Private practices tend to cluster—even in Chile, where they are not as numerous as in the United States or Canada. Physicians in the United States locate near high-income suburbanites, hospitals, and support facilities. Physician location in Canada (Rosenburg 1979) also indicates a clustered pattern. Private physicians in Santiago have become locationally more concentrated since 1950; despite efforts by the junta to enlist free-market measures. It seems, then, that the history of socialized medical care in Chile has made the spatial pattern of primary care somewhat resilient to changes in the larger political economy of the country.

Public clinics in the United States and Canada are sited by locational analysis or electoral demand. Public clinics in Chile, however, are located by the forces of spontaneous demand, public demand, and mayoral appeal. The efficacy of these procedures has been called into question under the authoritarian rule of the Pinochet government. The regressive nature of the current junta notwithstanding, nearest-neighbor analyses revealed that SNSS clinics are not randomly distributed, which suggests that perhaps spatial organization factors were considered in clinic location. The spatial distribution of clinics represents the culmination of a strong socialized medical system in Chile since 1952 and the advent of public medical programs since the second decade of this century.

Accessibility surfaces reveal that Santiago's western, central, and northern districts are better endowed than southern areas with public clinics. Upper-income neighborhoods in the northeast and low-income neighborhoods in the south had low indices of accessibility. Mapping exercises showed that low values of k (1.0 and 1.5) emphasize general effects of the distribution of clinics, and high values of k (2.5 and 3.0) highlight local conditions of accessibility. From a user's standpoint, higher values of k are better indices of overall accessibility because they offer a local appraisal of the supply of primary care. Conversely, planners at the Ministry of Health can use low values of k to assess regional conditions.

Local district health planners could use these measures to evaluate intradistrict and interdistrict variation in the utilization of SNSS clinics. Moreover, local district health planners could generate interaction models based on utilization figures for specialty services, such as well-baby clinics (*atención de niños sanos*), child and maternal care, infant formula programs, and alcohol abuse treatment. Socioeconomic data on the location and number of indigents could be used to identify clinics that are surrounded by extremely poor neighborhoods. However, this would require more complete and centralized collection of data by local municipalities, and both SNSS and health data collection has unfortunately become increasingly decentralized under junta rule.

FONASA general practitioners have concentrated in three clusters in the downtown area, while FONASA specialists are concentrated in the affluent *barrio alto*. It is hypothesized that both general practitioners and specialists locate near their clientele. There exists a strong and positive correlation between the location of private medical facilities and personal income in Santiago. Santiago municipality has a considerable number of general practitioners, while specialists concentrate in the amentity-rich *barrio alto*. A major difference between patterns of physician location in the United States and Santiago is that large suburban shopping centers are not a common feature in the latter.[13] Private physicians prefer aesthetically pleasing settings that are accessible by major transport arteries, such as the *Metro* and Providencia Avenue. The 1983 pattern of private medical doctors in Santiago is comparable to the immediate post-World War II period in the United States, when large shopping centers and shopping malls were scarce. The contemporary U.S. pattern of private physician locations is not likely to develop in Chile for two reasons. First, it is unlikely that a large enough clientele will emerge in Chile to support this industry. Second, there is an absence of commercial property on the scale required to accommodate large retail centers in northeastern Santiago.

Three lines of contemporary geographic thought were considered at the outset of this chapter in order to more fully interpret the spatial pattern of primary care in Santiago. The neoclassical perspective is represented by the empirical observations presented. Private physicians locate near their clientele and support facilities. Research by Arze (1984) is representative of the humanistic school, but such studies on Santiago are few. It would be fruitful to pursue more behavioral or humanistic inquires into the location of physicians in light of common patterns of physician spatial behavior in Canada and Chile. As Rosenberg comments, "in contrast to American research that shows physicians acting as entrepreneurs locating in higher income areas, [this] evidence adds weight to the belief that the basis for understanding the location of physicians in Canadian cities may be better understood using a behavioural approach" (1983b: 7).

A third perspective, that of the structuralist school, was also examined. A central line of thought here is that the state develops a medical system to rectify the inevitable weaknesses of the marketplace. Accordingly, SNSS primary care can be considered as one element of collective consumption that is provided to avoid a collapse in social relations. The state is also able to ensure a cheap and healthy pool of labor, a necessity for capitalist production. This research has not found that the poor are strongly discriminated against by the distribution of public clinics. Areas of underprovision were identified but not solely at the expense of poor areas of the city. SNSS users in older, more established, low-income areas in western and northern Santiago benefited from high potential accessibility. More refined analysis is needed to address this question further. Nonetheless, Castells' argument (1978) that state programs mitigate social tensions that might otherwise escalate to revolutionary movements seems particularly pertinent to the present Chilean experience. Accessible medical care is a key component in low- and middle-income groups' support of the Pinochet regime.

VI
Conclusion

The reduction of public medical care in Chile goes beyond a mere response to the fiscal crisis of mounting foreign debt and inflation, the drop in the demand for copper, and the poor international economic climate. At work is a major redefinition of the role of private medicine in the Chilean political economy that has triggered unprecedented investment in new medical programs. The fiscal crisis in the Chilean medical care sector reflects the pursuit of profit and the contradictions that derive from that effort. Tangible outcomes of these contradictions include smaller provider-population ratios, more expensive care for skilled workers who receive care under the FONASA, and the high level of investment in the private medical sector.

Operating under the premise that a minimum level of medical care should exist for the poor and working class, the authoritarian state has maintained a "safety net" of medical programs while encouraging investment in high-technology curative medical care. In neoclassical thinking, these new medical programs should foster competition, which in turn will make private medical care less expensive for a greater proportion of medical users. This is a free-market approach in its early stages: consumers are free to choose providers according to their preferences and purchasing power.

By adopting this model of medical care, the Pinochet regime naively accepts the idea that individual control and social independence can substantially replace primary care in a developing country. Such thinking is characteristic of the industralized capitalist nations, where individual health is largely a function of personal behavior and pathogens. To generalize this notion to Chile is unwise, because it assumes that the masses spend their leisure time and incomes in ways that produce most of their ill health and that socioeconomic conditions are secondary to pathogenic origins.

The restructured medical care financial system illustrates major differences between the way the Chilean junta conceptualizes medical care accessibility and availability and the way previous and more welfare-oriented administrations thought about them. Expanding *partially* state-financed medical care helps to foster private medical care alternatives. Witness, for example, the new laws that enable more private practitioners to work in the FONASA, the ISAPREs, and other private medical practices because of consumers' increased payroll deductions and more out-of-pocket payments. Thus the availability of providers has increased with no regard for the rather low purchasing power of the medical care consumer. These medical care policies have netted a decrease of 8 percentage points in the utilization of SNSS care, from 58 percent in 1977 to 50 percent in 1983, the privatization of some medical programs, and fiscal retrenchment across the board in the public medical sector. The regime's proposal to invest pension funds, in the midst of a waning economy and in the aftermath of a major setback of its monetarist policies, signals the avidity with which the present regime is willing to carry out its policies. The crucial matter, and one this research has attempted to address, is the influence that these changes have had and will have on medical care consumers.

The most formidable deterrent to care—financial cost—is affecting income groups differentially. FONASA consumers, the bulk of the middle-class medical market, have been the most adversely affected. FONASA's three levels of care illustrate a hierarchy of providers, with a larger number of them in the most expensive levels. In terms of relative accessibility, medical vouchers experienced the second greatest increase in the consumer price index during the third quarter of 1983. Perhaps the most telling sign of deteriorating medical care accessibility was the decline of the medical consumer price index by about one-fifth between 1978 and 1983. Once again, middle-income groups have borne the brunt of this increase, because blue-collar workers continue to receive free care. Wage and salary withholdings for medical care increased from 4 percent to 6 percent within two years, while real wages were falling. These financial trends indicate the extent to which Chileans are paying more for medical care under Pinochet's rule.

The SNSS, the largest provider of medical care in Chile, has also been weakened under the junta's rule. The proportion of users nationally has declined, not by consumer choice but by program decrees. Likewise, the SNSS physician-to-population ratio fell between 1970 and 1980. However, the contribution of worker and indigent payments to SNSS revenues has not exceeded 10 percent under the authoritarian rule of Pinochet, the socialist government of Allende, nor the Christian Democratic administration of Frel: no support can be found for the claim that the poor are contributing a greater proportion to the SNSS budget (through greater out-of-pocket charges at SNSS clinics) under military rule than under previous governments. Although medication and prostheses sales under the junta have been greater than under the Allende government, their relative contribution to the national medical care budget is comparable to the early years of the Frel and Alessandri governments. As is often the case with large national medical care systems throughout the world, the major cost incurred by consumers is measured by their long waiting time in queues.

Cultural and organizational barriers to primary care were few, as revealed in the study of 140 users of an SNSS clinic in southeastern Santiago. Conflict exists between auxiliary personnel and consumers but is absent in the patient-doctor relationship. It is likely that tensions between staff and patients and the lengthy wait at this clinic have been common features of the system since its inception in 1952. The perceived quality of care delivered by physicians was found to be slightly higher than the measures taken from other studies in Chile and points to a high degree of satisfaction among this clinic's users. Given the lack of affordable child-care facilities, women depend upon informal social networks to look after children or else children accompany women to the clinic. In an international context, women at this clinic experience fewer hindrances to primary medical care than many of their Latin American counterparts. Regardless of patients' gender, they associated physicians' touch with high-quality care. Because it is unlikely that any medical examination is carried out without some touching, this appraisal suggests the perception not only that the physicians were concerned but that they accepted and competently treated the patients.

Patients interviewed held a strong conviction that their medical care was a basic civil right. This was their main reason for coming to the Villa O'Higgins clinic, surpassing even geographic proximity. Although the majority of patients were legally entitled to care because of their indigence, their sense of correspondence with the SNSS went beyond a mere geographic assignment to a particular facility. This finding, along with patients' preference for public care (even if they had the money to purchase private primary medical care in the marketplace) has a significant policy implication. It reveals a deeply entrenched conviction that medical care coverage is a benefit inherent in their status as citizens. Moreover, it implies that about half of all Chileans will find further modifications to the SNSS delivery system unacceptable. The hypothetical point where medical services are too greatly curtailed may be the moment when the support of the current regime—already dwindling—subsides markedly, the state's role as a guarantor of a healthy labor force declines, and its control over the proletariat is dramatically challenged (Castells 1978). Ensured minimum levels of medical care accessibility may serve to quell some civil disorder until the end of Pinochet's rule in

1989 or 1996. Regardless of the longevity of the junta, the state medical system has proven to be more resistant to rapid dismantling than other state-run services and industries.

Geographic access to primary medical care was addressed by both the Villa O'Higgins survey and a study of the spatial organization of primary care facilities in Greater Santiago. The distribution of fifty-four SNSS clinics did not favor high- or middle-income districts of the city. Clinics have been set up amid neighborhood clusters that afford users low travel times. In the Villa O'Higgins survey, the median travel time was nine minutes, and the mean was about fourteen minutes. Eighty-five percent of the users interviewed made the trip by foot, in part because of proximity (the mean home-to-clinic vector distance was 0.7 kilometers), and in part because they lacked bus fare. The costs of travel in terms of time and money indicate the propinquity between clinic and users. The results obtained at Villa O'Higgins are not expected to vary widely from metropolitan averages.

Several indices of potential physical accessibility of the SNSS clinics were then examined. Various accessibility surfaces were generated by distance-decay parameters and a measure of physician hours provided. Not unexpectedly, these analyses indicated both areas of relative under- and overprovision of clinic accessibility. Low-income areas in Santiago experienced conflicting patterns of accessibility. Western Santiago municipalities, inhabited by a large portion of the urban poor, fared relatively well. On the other hand, southern municipalities exhibited low accessibility. This latter area is comprised of the municipalities of La Florida, La Granja, and La Cisterna and contains many of the low-income settlements (both legal and illegal) of Greater Santiago. Moreover, it is one of the few areas in Santiago where squatters have settled during the Pinochet rule. Its recent and fast growth may account for the relative underprovision of services there. An extension of SNSS operating hours into the late afternoon and early evening at selected facilities, implemented in 1984, could alter the 1983 accessibility patterns analyzed in this study.

In the private medical sector, a strong and positive relationship was detected between the number of private ambulatory and hospital facilities and mean family income. The locational patterns of general practitioners and specialists in Chile were compared to those of Canada and the United States. It was found that Chilean general practitioners clustered more in the downtown area where white-collar employees work. Unlike its North American counterparts, Chile has few large-scale shopping facilities in the suburbs and relies less on automobile travel than on public transportation, which accounts for this deviation. More significant, however, was the finding that, unlike private physicians in the United States, where the private medical market has acted as an agent of dispersal, those in Santiago are locationally more concentrated. This observation reveals a similarity to the Rosenberg study (1983b) on physician location in Toronto: socialized medical systems disperse physicians less than free-market settings. Coefficients of localization in Santiago from 1950 to 1980 showed that physicians have become locationally more concentrated in recent times. Both the historical trend of private physician concentration and the 1983 location patterns among FONASA and private medical centers will provide good indications of the changing urban and medical geography of Santiago as privatization efforts continue.

Evaluations of health care in any setting are difficult, and the Chilean case proves to be no exception. Government publications have repeatedly emphasized that the institutional aspects of medical care are well founded in light of the continuing decline in infant mortality. But major questions linger. First, can a single administration be wholly responsible for the decline in infant mortality? And even if that were true, can it then be assumed that the quality of life has improved? As was argued in chapter 2, death is a poor outcome measure of both the quality of medical care and the quality of life. The mental health needs of the country under authoritarian rule have been sadly neglected by researchers out of fear of reprisal from the armed forces. The regime has used fear and intimidation, curfews, and internal and foreign exile as mechanisms of social control. Few formal public services are available to family members, friends, and victims of these abuses. Perversely, an entire generation of Chileans has been raised under military rule where basic civil liberties have been denied at very significant psychological costs (Pollarola 1983). Data on referrals for mental health care at the primary level were unavailable, and therefore they have not been considered in this analysis. Nonetheless, this component of medical care is vital and will undoubtedly receive greater attention with the return of a democratic state in Chile.

At the outset, this research identified a shift in the political economy of Western capitalist nations. This new political economy hinges on the notion of less government participation in the provision of social services and a concomitant reduction of the public tax burden. This fiscal retrenchment, through a variety of mechanisms, has operated in the Chilean medical system under the Pinochet regime. While attempts to dismantle the welfare state may be more acceptable in countries with more equitable income distributions, it is incompatible with the income disparities, health status, and history of socialized medicine found in Chile. The traditional medical care system devoted to the general public good is being replaced by one that treats medical care as a private commodity. Although a return to democratic rule will not eliminate all of the inequities of the Chilean medical systems, it would allow the electorate to evaluate the adequacy of medical care accessibility under the restructured political economy of military rule.

Appendices

Notes

Literature Cited

Index

Variables from Villa O'Higgins Questionnaire

Variable	Definition
ABLEMEN	Males over fourteen years of age and not studying
ABLEWOM	Women over fourteen years of age and not studying
ADULTS	Number of adults in household
AGE	Age of patient
CLINBAR	Clinic-imposed barriers or difficulties
CLINCAMB	Number of clinic changes in last five years
CLINLIKE	Liked anything about clinic
DEPRATE	Dependency ratio: number of young and old divided by household size
DISLIKE	Disliked anything about clinic
DOCPREF	Prefers specific physician
DOCSELEC	Able to see preferred physician
DRUGTEST	Receipt of drug or test cited as reason for good care
EASECARE	Easy or difficult to get care
FARMUSE	Uses pharmacy as source of care
FEMHEAD	Patient is member of female-headed household
FEMINFOR	Number of women working in informal sector of economy
FOODEXP	Household monthly food expenditures
FOODPER	Household food expenditures per person
FREQVIS	Number of visits to clinic in past year

Variable	*Definition*
GOODCARE	Doctor-related attribute cited in appraisal of care
GOTDRUG	Prescription or laboratory test ordered at visit
HERBUSE	Uses herbal remedies
HHSIZE	Household size
HHMOINC	Household monthly income
HOSPITAL	Ever hospitalized
IFBUCS	Prefer private doctor if had money
KIDCARE	Child-care concerns
KILOM	Vector distance between residence and clinic
LIFCYC	Life-cycle measure: presence of children under five years of age in household
MENINFOR	Number of men working in informal sector of economy
MENSTDNT	Number of men over fourteen years of age and studying
MOMKID	Mother who brought child for medical visit
NIÑA	Number of girls under fourteen years of age in household
NIÑO	Number of boys under fourteen years of age in household
PEMMEN	Male workers in state program
PEMWOM	Female workers in state program
PERCAP	Per person household income
PERPOOR	Percentage poor in user's neighborhood
POSTA	Patient has been attended at first-aid station
PREFPRIV	Prefers private physician care
PRIVDOC	Patient has been attended by private physician
PROXIM	Patient claims to live close to or far from clinic
QUALCARE	Patient's evaluation of care (very good, good, fair, bad, very bad)
SEX	Gender of patient
STAFCAMB	Thought clinic staff changed often
SUGGEST	Offered a suggestion for improving clinic operations

Variable	*Definition*
TRAVTIME	Travel time to clinic
TIMEILL	Chronic-care or acute-care patient
WAITIME	Waiting time prior to physician examination
WHYDELAY	Reason for patient delay in seeking care
WOMSTDNT	Number of women over fourteen years of age and studying
WORKRATE	Ratio of adult workers in household to total number of adults

APPENDIX *B*
Spanish-Language Questionnaire

Hombre ___ Mujer ___ Dirección _____ Edad ___

1. ¿A cuántas cuadras del consultorio vive Ud.?

2. ¿Es cerca o lejos?

3. ¿Cuánto se demoró al llegar al consultorio?

4. ¿Como llegó al consultorio?
    a. a pie
    b. por bicicleta
    c. por micro o liebre
    d. por taxi
    e. por auto privado

5. ¿Es fácil para Ud. conseguir atención?

6. ¿A qué hora tuvo que llegar para conseguir atención?

7. ¿Cuándo se enfermó?

8. Si se enfermó antes, ¿Por qué no vino antes?
    a. problemas de trabajo
    b. nadie para cuidar a los niños
    c. la enfermedad se empeoró
    d. vino antes pero no le atendieron

148

e. probó remedios caseros
f. probó remedios de la farmacia

9. ¿Qué dificultades le puso el consultorio para conseguir atención médica?
   a. tramites con la asistente social
   b. certificado de residencia
   c. certificado de previsión
   d. pago/cobro
   e. otro

10. Siempre que se enferma, ¿viene al consultorio? ¿Por qué?

11. ¿Ha ido alguna vez a un médico particular? ¿Por qué?

12. ¿Prefiere ir a un médico particular? ¿Por qué?

13. Asi que si tuviera más dinero, ¿preferiría ir a un médico particular? ¿Por qué?

14. ¿Cuánto gana la familia al mes?

15. ¿Cuánto dispone para "la olla" al mes?

16. ¿Quién queda cuidando a los hijos cuando viene al consultirio?
   a. vecinos
   b. ellos solos
   c. esposo(a)
   d. otro pariente
   e. no aplicable

17. ¿Qué le desagrada más de este consultorio?

18. ¿Qué le agrada más de este consultorio?

19. ¿Cambian mucho los doctores y las enfermeras aquí?

20. ¿Cuántas veces ha cambiado de consultorio en los últimos cinco años?

21. ¿Se puede atender con el médico que Ud. quiere que le atienda?

22. ¿Le gustaría que el médico que Ud. prefiere le atienda?

23. ¿Cuánto tiempo tuvo que esperar hasta que lo atendieran?

24. ¿Diría Ud. que la atención médica fue muy buena, buena, regular, mala, o muy mala?

25. ¿Por qúe fue la atención asi?

26. ¿Le recetaron remedios? ¿Dónde piensa obtenerlos?

27. ¿Le pidieron examenes? ¿Dónde piensa hacérselos?

28. ¿Cuántas veces ha venido Ud. a este consultorio en el año?

29. ¿Ha recibido Ud. otro tipo de atención en alguno de los siguientes lugares?
   a. consultorio
   b. médico particular
   c. posta de urgencia
   d. hospital

30. ¿Ha sido Ud. tratado en los últimos dos años por alguna enfermedad grave? ¿Cuál(es)?

31. ¿Ha usado Ud. otros remedios recetados por Ud. mismo/a o los vecinos? ¿Cuáles hierbas? ¿Cuáles cosas de la farmacia?

32. ¿Qué mejoras sugeriría Ud. para que este consultorio sea más efectivo?

APPENDIX C
English-Language Translation of Questionnaire

Man ___ Woman ___ Address _____Age ___

1. How many blocks from the clinic do you live?

2. Is that nearby or far away?

3. How long did it take you to arrive at the clinic?

4. How did you get to the clinic?
    a. foot
    b. bicycle
    c. bus
    d. taxi
    e. private car

5. Is it easy or difficult to get care?

6. What time did you have to get to the clinic?

7. When did you become ill?

8. If you fell ill before today, why didn't you come sooner?
    a. work problems
    b. child-care problems
    c. sickness worsened
    d. came but wasn't attended

e. took home remedies
f. got remedies from drug store

9. What difficulties did the clinic place on you to get care?
    a. runaround by social worker
    b. residence certification
    c. health care certification
    d. payment or charges
    e. other

10. Do you always come to the clinic when you get sick? Why?

11. Have you ever gone to a private doctor? Why?

12. Do you prefer to go to a private doctor? Why?

13. If you had more money would you prefer to see a private physician? Why?

14. How much does the family or household earn monthly?

15. How much does that leave you for food?

16. Who takes care of the kids when you come to the clinic?
    a. neighbors
    b. themselves
    c. spouse
    d. other relative
    e. not applicable

17. What do you dislike most about this clinic?

18. What do you like most about this clinic?

19. Do the doctors and nurses change often here?

20. How many times have you changed clinics in the last five years?

21. Is it possible for the doctor of your choice to treat you?

22. Would you like the doctor of your choice to treat you?

23. How long did you have to wait until you were attended?

24. Would you say that the medical care was very good, good, fair, bad, or very bad?

25. Why was the care that way?

26. Did you get a prescription? Where will you get it filled?

27. Will they take tests? Where will you have them done?

28. How many times this year have you come to the clinic?

29. Have you gotten care in any of the following places?
    a. other clinic
    b. private doctor
    c. first aid station
    d. hospital

30. Have you been treated in the last two years for a serious illness? Which?

31. Have you used other types of treatment prescribed by you or your neighbors? Which herbs? Which items from the pharmacy?

32. What improvements would you suggest to make the clinic more effective?

APPENDIX *D*

Glossary of Spanish Words and Acronyms

AFPs	*Administradoras de fondos de pensión* (pension fund administrators). Since 1981 these agencies have been funded by monthly wage deductions and can be selected by Chileans as both a retirement and medical care fund. Unused funds acrue interest. In 1984 there was speculation that the state would place these monies in capital-generating investment plans, even though depositors would be insured against any loss.
barrio alto	Upper-income neighborhoods. In Greater Santiago, these are the municipalities of Providencia and Las Condes.
bono	A medical voucher issued by the FONASA. Several vouchers are usually required for the delivery of therapeutic and curative care. Three price levels of vouchers existed under the FONASA in 1983. Vouchers were also used under the SERMENA.
consultorios periféricos	Public medical clinics administered by the SNSS or local municipalities. These primary care facilities are staffed by physicians and are located in urban centers throughout Chile. Each *consultorio* is affiliated with a

hospital. There were sixty-four SNSS *consultorios* in Greater Santiago in 1983.

cotización
Monthly wage and salary withholdings placed in a public or private medical care system of the users' choice.

centro médico
Private medical centers, usually with both ambulatory and in-patient care. The latter usually have fewer than fifty beds.

Colegio Médico
The Chilean Medical Society. It is the largest professional organization of physicians in the country. Until 1979, membership was obligatory for all practicing physicians, but since then affiliation has been on a voluntary basis.

empleado
A middle-income white-collar worker whose major source of medical care is usually the FONASA.

FAP
Factura de atención prestada. Reimbursement charge for primary care sent by *consultorio* to the FONASA.

FONASA
Fondo Nacional de Salud (the National Health Fund), called SERMENA until 1980. The FONASA provides three levels of comprehensive medical care, differentiated by the cost of medical vouchers (*bonos*), to public and private middle-income workers. Under administrative reorganization in 1980, the FONASA now administers all medical care funds from the state that are directed to the Ministry of Health and the SNSS.

INE
Instituto Nacional de Estadísticas (National Statistics Institute).

ISAPREs

Institutos de salud previsional (provisional health institutes). A form of prepaid private medical care modeled after the health maintenance organizations (HMOs) of the United States. The ISAPREs were introduced in 1981, although a few somewhat similar organizations existed in Chile under the name *cajas*.

junta de vecinos

Neighborhood boards. Voluntary organizations that monitor community issues and needs. Requests for health clinics, police and fire protection, and other public services are passed on from these organizations to the municipal authorities, who then forward the requests to the national ministerial levels of government. In 1983 there were about a thousand of these organizations in Greater Santiago.

SERMENA

Servicio Médico Nacional de Empleados, (National Medical Service for Employees). Begun in 1938 to provide primary, secondary, and tertiary care to certain public workers. In 1968 nongovernmental workers were permitted to enroll. As the predecessor of the FONASA until 1980, it operated with medical care vouchers at two levels of care.

SNS

Servicio Nacional de Salud (National Health Service), created in 1952 as a central public agency to coordinate a number of public and private medical care systems serving blue-collar workers (obreros) and the medically indigent.

SNSS

Sistema Nacional del Servicio de Salud (National Health Service System), successor to the SNS. It is the largest medical network in the country and operates a hierarchy of services ranging from rural health stations (*postas rurales*) and urban clinics (*consultorios*) to hospitals.

Notes

Chapter 1. Introduction

1. Under the Carter administration, human rights abuses committed by the security forces of the Pinochet government were greatly curtailed. In the 1980s, under a waning economy and considerable opposition to the military government's rule, human rights abuses began to increase once again. For partial documentation, see Amnesty International Publications (1983).

An indication of the Reagan administration's tacit approval of the Pinochet regime and, indeed, other authoritarian governments, is borne out by comments made by President Reagan on national television during his October 1984 debate with former Vice President Walter Mondale. The President was asked by panelist Mr. Kondracke, "there are other such leaders heading for touble, including President Pinochet of Chile and President Marcos of the Philippines. What should you, and what can you, do to prevent the Philippines from becoming another Nicaragua?" Although the question was directed to the Philippine case, the response is equally germane to the Pinochet government. President Reagan responded, "I know there are things there in the Philippines that do not look good to us from the standpoint, right now, of democratic rights. But what is the alternative? It is a large communist movement to take over the Philippines. . . . And I think that we've had enough of a record of letting, under the guise of revolution, someone that we thought was a little more right than we would be, letting that person go and then winding up with totalitarianism, pure and simple, as the alternative. And I think that we're better off, for example, with the Philippines, of trying to retain our friendship and help them right the wrongs we see, rather than throwing them to the wolves and then facing a communist power in the Pacific" (*Congressional Quarterly* 1984: 2835–36).

Chapter 2. The Restructuring of Medical Care Financing in Chile

1. For an elaboration of this point, see Navarro (1976). One of Navarro's arguments is that the whole basis for the capitalist state's existence is to

service the diswelfare that the means of production creates. In the Chilean case, however, Navarro gives little attention to the performance of public-sector medical care under the governments before Allende (see Reidy 1984: 897–910, especially 907–09).

2. The Southern Cone encompasses the southern portion of South America and is also sometimes referred to as the "ABC countries"—Argentina, southern Brazil, Chile, and Uruguay.

3. Per capita national debt figures derived for the leading debtor nations in Latin America are: Venezuela, $1,738; Chile, $1,507; Argentina, $1,374; Costa Rica, $1,235; and Mexico, $1,132. Population data for computing per capita debt are taken from *Boletín Demográfico* 16 (1983): 2. Foreign debt totals come from preliminary 1983 figures in *Sintesis Preliminar de la Economía Latinoamericana durante 1983*, Santiago: United Nations Economic Council, 1984, p. 44.

4. Chile's Ministry of Health has stated to the press on numerous occasions that a major survey of users of public-sector medical programs was carried out in 1983. To the author's knowledge, however, the survey design and printed findings have not been disclosed. The author was denied a copy of the survey results, one of only two occasions that requests for information from a public agency were turned down in fourteen months of fieldwork.

5. See various editions of the Santiago daily newspaper *El Mercurio*, especially the section Economía y Negocios, April 1, 3, 11, and 18, 1984.

6. The ministers of Health in Chile since the overthrow of the Allende government are: Colonel Alfredo Spoerer (November 1973); Dr. Francisco Herrera Latoja (1974 to February 1976); General Fernando Matthei (March 1976 to July 1978); Carlos Mario Jiménez Vargas (August 1978 to December 1979); General Alejandro Medina Lois (December 1979 to March 1981); Admiral Hernán Rivera Calderón (March 1981 to August 1983); Dr. Winston Chinchón (August 1983 to August 1986; and Dr. Juan Giaconi Gandolfo (August 1986 to —). I am grateful to reference librarian Maria Teresa Astroza, Pan American Health Organization, Washington, D.C., for researching this information, but I assume responsibility for any inaccuracies.

7. See, for example, *El Mercurio* 1984a, 1984b, 1984c.

8. Although the changes that have been enacted in Chile are far more sweeping than the health and social policy changes in the United States, the similarities are evident. See the final chapter of Starr (1982: especially 417–19).

Chapter 3. *Inflation and Medical Care Accessibility*

1. It is difficult to cite specified population-resource ratios for the use of CAT scanners and other medical equipment, even in the United States where these resources are common. One way to estimate equipment level is the number of procedures per thousand inhabitants. This crude estimate, derived by the

Leonard methodology, was 4.35 for the North Central Florida region (personal communication: letter from J. N. Gregg, 22 May 1985, North Central Florida Health Planning council).

2. The author observed that working-class Chileans had more gold dental work than those in higher-income classes. The use of gold in dental prostheses is common in Chile and is likely to be considered a superior good among some groups.

Chapter 4. Help-Seeking Behavior of the Urban Poor

1. Given an estimated service population of 35 thousand users, the selection of a representative sample is as follows:

$$n_o = t^2\, pq/d^2,$$

where

n_o = estimate of sample size,
t = number of standard errors which lie within the confidence intervals,
p = proportion of population having one characteristic,
q = proportion of population having the second characteristic, and
d^2 = the acceptable error limit.

Since the number of residents who rely on Villa O'Higgins as a regular source of care is not known, the sample is maximized by setting the proportion to 50 percent. Applying the formula is as follows:

$n_o = 1.96^2\ (.50 \times .50)/.085^2,$
$n_o = 3.84\ (.25)/.00723,$
$n_o = .9604/.00723,$
$n_o = 132.84.$

Thus a sample of 133 patients was selected at the 91.5 percent confidence level (see Dever, 1980: 152–54).

2. This significance level $(p < .001)$ indicates that there is one chance out of 1,000 that the null hypothesis set up for this correlation test, stating that there are no statistically significant associations between monthly household income and the number of working men and women in the household, should be rejected when in fact it is true. Put another way, there is just one chance in 1,000 that the strength of the correlation between the two variables is a function of sampling error, producing spurious results.

3. Although the correlation coefficient for the number of working men is greater than the coefficient for the number of working women, a z-test outlined by Agresti and Agresti (1979: 318–19) revealed that the correlation values are not significantly different from each other.

4. The Comite de Acción Social (CAS) is a standard of living survey coordinated by the Ministry of the Interior and carried out by municipal governments. The survey is a measure of the physical conditions of homes and does not include questions of income. Persons wishing housing subsidies and free medical care may have to submit to a household survey. Responses are weighted and produce a summary score of standard of living, which is then divided into five groups. Those households with scores in the first three groups are classified as "extremely poor" and are able to receive state benefits. The PERPOOR variable used in this study measures the percentage of poor according to the CAS data.

5. A chi-square test revealed no statistically significant differences between hospitalization and nonhospitalization or male and female.

6. A number of possible translations exist for *me corresponde* and *me pertenece*. Given the intonation in the voice and the strong affirmation in responding to the question about why they came to the clinic, it seems safe to take a figurative translation of the responses. Literally, their answers were "I belong here" or "I am assigned here." but when the phrase *me corresponde* or *me pertenece* is used in Chile and it refers to social programs, it usually implies that a service is legally condoned and the individual is a designated beneficiary.

7. Comparative figures are difficult to cite because this study surveyed only users. A recent health survey did find that Santiago residents who claimed the SNSS as their regular source of care averaged 0.98 visits per year (Medina n.d.: 28).

8. U.S. standards regarding waiting time for primary care (except in emergency rooms) are clearly not comparable. What is evident throughout the Chilean medical system, as in other socialized medical systems, is the complacency among users. Long waits become a norm and a cost that the user must pay.

9. Given the importance that spatial variables have played in international medical care studies (Kohn and White 1976), a further test was incorporated to assess the strength of the correlation between travel time (TRAVTIME) and the ease by which care is obtained (EASECARE). Because the product-moment correlation is best suited for continuous variables, the point-biserial correlation method was used to test TRAVTIME and EASECARE. The point-biserial correlation technique is an appropriate test when one variable is continuous (TRAVTIME) and the other is dichotomous (EASECARE; Isaac and Michael 1981: 168–72). Its computation considers the mean travel time for those who found care to be easily obtainable (M = 11.5 minutes) and for those who did not (M = 15.9 minutes). A point-biserial correlation coefficient of $-.192$ (p = .05) indicates that the strength of the relationship between the two variables was not as strong as originally thought. Both the product-moment and point-biserial correlation methods are measures of statistical association and not

causality. They are discussed in greater detail in the following section, which discusses models of the use of and satisfaction with care.

10. The logarithm of FREQVIS was employed because of several high values, which greatly skewed the data.

11. Predicted proportional change is derived by multiplying the variance of the dependent variable by the full model coefficient. Chi-square measures in logit models represent twice the difference in the log likelihood of the present model from the likelihood that would be generated based only on the intercept. As such, it can be interpreted like the ratio chi-square found more commonly among simple 2×2 contingency tables when a binary variable is present.

12. Patients were familiar with a number of brand names and frequently cited Brazilian, German, Swiss, and U.S. pharmaceutical brands. They claimed that these foreign brands were better than Chilean ones. The commercialization of medical products among the urban poor of Santiago is such that, although many did not know the name of the physician who had just treated them, they readily recalled the brand name of the prescription or the name of the pharmaceutical company.

13. It is possible that "touching" was listed under another rubric, but this is not apparent in the headings used by Cartwright (1967: 5–7).

Chapter 5. *Spatial Organization and Medical Care Accessibility*

1. Sixty-four clinics providing care to an average of 47 thousand users would include 3,008,280 Santiagoans, or 68.4 percent of the Greater Santiago population of 4,200,000. This is comparable to the Ministry of Health estimate that about 70 percent of the metropolitan population receives care from these *consultorios periféricos*.

2. The Pinochet regime has been less tolerant than previous administrations of these land invasions. They are seen as highly illegal acts as well as a reminder of the Allende period, when they were commonplace.

3. There exists in many spatial statistical measures a boundary effect, which refers to the distance from outer areal limits to all points. The areal boundary can determine whether patterns are described as clustered or dispersed. Silk cautions that "boundaries should be drawn in a manner consistent with the subject matter under investigation. . . . If the points represent retail outlets, the study should include all contiguous built-up areas at the edge of the city, and not simply follow administrative boundaries. Ideally, boundaries should be placed *within* the outermost limits of the study area" (1979: 110). Boundary selection is an important component in generating accurate nearest-neighbor values. For example, if a larger study area is defined about a small, regularly spaced pattern of points, then the calculated value of R will suggest a clustered pattern (Taylor 1977: 166).

4. Donnely's adjustment measure for the boundary effect was applied (see Aplin 1983). Values of R reported here are adjusted by the measure

$$[(.5)(NA)^{.5} + (.051) + (.041N)^{-.5L}],$$

where

    N is the number of points,
    A is the area encompassing the points, and
    L is the perimeter of the area.

5. The z-tests described by Silk (1979) and Aplin (1983) were applied. In general, Silk's measure is more appropriate when the number of points exceeds 50. Both tests were used here, since $N = 54$. First-order z-test values were -2.64 and -3.15 according to Silk's and Aplin's forumulae, respectively. Second-order z-test scores for Silk and Aplin z-values were 2.84 and 2.06, respectively. Interpretation of second-order neighbor analysis is less straightforward because, visually, it is difficult to sense the proximity of each point to its second-nearest point.

6. The distance-decay function in modeling medical care delivery is an assessment of the hypothetical impact that distance will have on use. Use (or interaction) can decline as distance increases but at a decreasing ratio (called a hybrid function). A distance-decay function of 2, for example, indicates a steady decline in accessibility with an additional increase in distance from a point. For a review of the specification of distance-decay functions and parameters see Morrill and Kelley (1970).

7. A value of 1.0 is frequently used in specifying distance-decay parameters *(k)*. Knox (1979, 1978) used a value of 1.55 derived from data used by Hopkins et al. (1968). This parameter was generated from a regression model of the falloff rate in clinic attendance among a sample of British facilities. In this Santiago study, a regression model predicting a distance-decay parameter produced a value of 1.48.

8. The translation for critical care medicine is taken from the Spanish term *cuidado intensivo*. Literally, it translates as "intensive care." But U.S. physicians working in critical or intensive care units tend to be unit directors who are anesthesiologists. In Chile, this medical specialty is best described as critical care medicine. It is most common in large teaching or public hospitals. The author is grateful to Stephanie Tison, R.N., of Alachua General Hospital, and Mark Walsh, R.T., of the Veterans Hospital, Gainesville, Florida, for their clarification of this term.

9. In the examination of the relationship between the location of private medical centers and the economic status of the municipality where they are located, normal income distribution could not be assumed. Thus the nonparametric Spearman's rank-correlation test was used. The Spearman procedure is 91 percent as powerful as the Pearson product-moment correlation test (Hammond and McCullagh 1974).

10. Joseph (1982) has found the coefficient of localization to be sensitive to the underlying population distribution. In addition, the coefficient of localization measures concentration relative to a base magnitude and is not a measure of absolute concentration (see Joseph and Phillips 1984, Joseph 1982, and Isard 1960 for an in-depth review of the strengths and weaknesses of the measure). The results in this Santiago study are influenced by the presence of only one doctor in Las Condes in 1950, and a twenty-eight-fold increase by 1980. Also, the results are based on population and physician concentrations within five core municipalities. Although a larger data set might generate different results, the five municipalities are included because they encompass the effective private medical sector.

11. Medical indigents are those persons who cannot afford complete medical care but who are not necessarily indigent according to nationally defined poverty levels (see Pyle 1979).

12. It should be noted that although Rosenberg concluded that physicians' locations in Toronto are becoming less concentrated, the nearest-neighbor value of R changed only form .327 in 1951 to .481 in 1971 (Rosenberg 1983b: 5). Such low R-values denote a very clustered pattern in both time periods.

13. There was one large shopping mall in Greater Santiago in 1983, *Parque Arauco*, located in the municipality of Las Condes.

Literature Cited

Aday, L., and Andersen, R. 1975. *Development of Indices of Access to Medical Care.* Ann Arbor: Health Administration Press.

Aday, L.; Andersen, R.; and Fleming, G. 1980. *Health Care in the U.S.* Beverly Hills: Sage.

Agresti, A., and Agresti, B. F. 1979. *Statistical Methods for the Social Sciences.* San Francisco: Dellen.

Akin, J. S.; Guilkey, D. K.; Griffin, C. C.; and Popkin, B. M. 1985. *The Demand for Primary Health Services in the Third World.* Totowa, NJ: Rowman and Allenheld.

Amato, P. W. 1970. La evolución, ratificación oficial y consecuencias del uso de las tierras en una ciudad latinoamericana. *Revista Ciencias Sociales* 14:397–414.

Amnesty International Publications. 1983. *Chile, Evidence of Torture.* London: AIP.

Anderson, O. W. 1972. *Health Care: Can There Be Equity? The U.S., Sweden, and England.* New York: Wiley.

Anthony, H. 1979. *The Challenge of Squatter Settlements: Special Reference to Latin America.* Vancouver: University of British Columbia.

Antonovsky, A. 1979. Implications of socioeconomic differentials in mortality for the health service system. Paper presented at the World health Organization meeting on socioeconomic determinants and consequenes of mortality, Mexico City, 19–25 June. Mimeo.

Aplin, G. 1983. *Order-Neighbour Analysis.* Catmog 36. Norwich, U.K.: Geo Books.

Arroba, G. 1979. La financiación de la seguridad social en los paises en desarrollo. *Estudios de Seguridad Social* 29:5–31.

Arze, A. M. 1984. Cambios en la localización de oficinas prividas de las profesiones liberales en Santiago entre los años 1950 y 1980. Bachelor's thesis, Catholic University of Chile.

Baehr, G. 1966. Prepaid group practice: its strengths and weaknesses, and its future. *American Journal of Public Health* 56:1889–1904.

Bähr, J. 1978. Santiago de Chile. *Mannheimer Geographische Arbeiten* 4. Mannheim, Germany.

Bähr, J., and Mertins, G. 1982. A model of the spatial differentiation of Latin American metropolitan cities. *Applied Geography and Development* 19:22–45.

Bähr, J., and Riesco, R. 1981. Estructura urbana de las metropolis latinoamericanas: El caso de la ciudad de Santiago. *Norte Grande* 8:27–56.

Barret, A. 1980. Canadian Studies in Medical Geography, Monograph no. 8. Department of Geography, York University, Toronto.

Basch, P. F. 1978. *International Health*. New York: Oxford University Press.

Behm, H. 1979. Socioeconomic determinants of mortality in Latin America. Paper presented at World Health Organization meeting on socioeconomic determinants and consequences of mortality, Mexico City, 19–25 June. Mimeo.

Belmar, Roberto, et al. 1977. Evaluation of Chile's health care system: A communique from health workers in Chile. *International Journal of Health Services* 7:531–40.

Benson, J., and McClave, R. 1982. *Statistics for Business and Economics*. San Francisco: Dellen.

Benyoussef, A. 1977. Monitoring and servicing national health service delivery in developing countries. *International Social Science Journal* 29:397–419.

Berg, A. 1973. *The Nutrition Factor: Its Role in National Development*. Washington, DC: Brookings.

Bice, T. W., and White, K. L. 1971. Cross-national comparative research and the utilization of medical care. *Medical Care* 9:253–71.

Blishen, B. R. 1969. *Doctors and Doctrines: The Ideology of Medical Care in Canada*. Toronto: University of Toronto Press.

Boland, R., and Young, M. 1983. ¿A qué precio la atención primaria de salud? *Foro Mundial de Salud* 4:151–54.

Borgoño, J.; Dominguez, N.J.; Aldea, A.; and Acuña, C. 1983. Condiciones de eficiencia de los consultorios periféricos de atención materno-infantil. *Cuadernos Médico-Sociales* 24:13–24.

Bottomley, J. 1971. Physician office site characteristics: A cognitive-behaviorial approach. Master's thesis, University of British Columbia.

Brown, L. A., and Belcher, J. C. 1966. Residential mobility of physicians in Georgia. *Rural Sociology* 31:439–48.

Brown, L., and Lawson, V. 1985. Migration in Third World settings: Uneven development and conventional modeling. *Annals of the Association of American Geographers* 75:29–47.

Buckner, Ted. 1985. BASIC software program of order-neighbor analysis. Gainesville: Department of Geography, University of Florida.

Burstein, P. L., and Cromwell, J. 1985. Relative incomes and rates of returns for U.S. physicians. *Journal of Health Economics* 4:63–78.

Busch, L., and Dale, C. 1978. The changing distribution of physicians. *Socio-economic Planning Sciences* 12:167–76.

Buttimer, A. 1976. Grasping the dynamism of lifeworld. *Annals of the Association of American Geographers* 66:277–92.

Calvo, A. B., and Marks, D. H. 1973. Location of health care facilities: An analytical approach. *Socio-economic Planning Sciences* 7:407–22.

Cartwright, A. 1967. *Patients and Their Doctors: A Study of General Practice*. New York: Atherton.

de Carvalho, J. A. M., and Wood, C. H. 1978. Mortality, income distribution, and rural-urban residence in Brazil. *Population and Development Review* 4:405–20.

Castells, M. 1978. *City, Class and Power*. London: Macmillan.

Castillo, B.; Solis, F.; and Mardones, G. 1982. Influencias del sector salud en los niveles de la mortalidad infantil chilena. In *Infant and Child Mortality in the Third World*. Paris: WHO.

Caviedes, C. N. 1979. *The Politics of Chile: A Sociogeographical Assessment*. Boulder, Co: Westview.

———. 1984. *The Southern Cone*. Totowa, NJ: Rowman and Allanheld.

Chanfreau, D. 1979. Professional ideology and the health care system in Chile. *International Journal of Health Services* 9:86–105.

Colegio Médico. 1981. ISAPREs. *Vida Médica* June-July:12–27.

———. 1983a. Algunas consideraciones sobre la salud en Chile.

———. 1983b. Medicina curativa en crisis. *Vida Médica* April: 12–19.

———. 1983c. Derechos laborales perdidos por los medicos funcionarios en el SNSS. Santiago, 1 July.

———. 1984. Algunas consideraciones sobre la salud en Chile. July 1.

Collier, D. 1976. *Squatters and Oligarchs: Authoritarian Rule and Policy Change in Peru*. New York: Johns Hopkins University Press.

Congressional Quarterly. 1984. October 27.

Cortázar, R. 1983. Chile: Resultados distributivos, 1973–82. *Notas Tecnicas* 57. CIEPLAN.

Cortázar, R., and Marshall, J. 1980. Indice del precio al consumidor en Chile: 1970–1980. *Colección Estudios CIEPLAN* 4 (November).

Covarrubias, P., and Franco, R. 1978. *Chile: Mujer y Sociedad*. Santiago: Fondo de las Naciones Unidas para la Infancia.

Cruz-Coke, R. 1983. Los profesores de la escuela de medicina y la historia política nacional (1833–1973). *Revista Médica de Chile* 111:380–87.

Cugliani, A. 1978. Patterns of hospital-based ambulatory care. *Social Science and Medicine* 12:55–58.

Davis, T. E. 1963. Eight decades of inflation in Chile: A political interpretation. *Journal of Political Economy* 71:389–97.

Deodhar, N.S. 1982. Primary health care in India. *Journal of Public Health Policy* 3:76–99.

Derbyshire, R. 1969. *Medical Licensure and Discipline in the United States.* Baltimore: Johns Hopkins University Press.

de Vise, P. 1973. *Misused and Misplaced Hospitals and Doctors: A Locational Analysis of the Urban Health Care Crisis.* Resource Paper no. 22. Washington, DC: Association of American Geographers.

Dever, G. E. A. 1980. *Community Health Analysis: A Holistic Approach.* Germantown, MD: Aspen.

Dewey, D. 1973. *Where Have the Doctors Gone?* Chicago: Illinois Regional Medical Program.

Donabedian, A. 1973. *Needed Aspects of Medical Care Administration.* Cambridge, MA: Harvard University Press.

———. 1980. *The Definition of Quality and Approaches to Its Assessment.* Vol. 1. Ann Arbor: Health Administration Press.

Dougenik, J. A., and Sheehan, D. E. 1979. *SYMAP User's Guide.* Cambridge, MA: Laboratory for Computer Graphics and Spatial Analysis, Harvard University.

Doyal, L., and Pennell, I. 1979. *The Political Economy of Health Care.* Boston: South End Press.

Earickson, R. 1970. *The Spatial Behavior of Hospital Patients.* Research Paper 124. Chicago: Department of Geography, University of Chicago.

Economist. 1985. Profitable American hospitals. 18 May.

Elbow, G. 1983. Determinants of land use change in Guatemalan secondary urban centers. *Professional Geographer* 35:57–65.

Elling, R. H. 1981. The fiscal crisis of the state and state financing of health care. *Social Science and Medicine* 15C:207–17.

Enthoven, A. 1981. The competition strategy: Status and Prospects. *New England Journal of Medicine* 304:109–12.

Ercilla (Santiago). 1980. Marcha de capas blancas. 26 March.

Ernst, R. L., and Yett, D. E. 1985. *Physician Location and Specialty and Choice.* Ann Arbor, MI: Health Administration Press.

Etten, G., and Rutten, F. 1983. Health policy and health services research in the Netherlands. *Social Science and Medicine* 17:119–26.

Facts on File. 1978. New York: FOF.

Fainstein, N. I., and Fainstein, S. S., eds. 1982. *Urban Policy Under Capitalism.* Beverly Hills: Sage.

Falkson, J. L. 1981. Market reform, health systems, and HMOs. *Policy Studies Journal* 9:213–20.

Fausto, D., and Leccisotti, M. 1981. An interpretation of government intervention in health: The Italian case. In *Health, Economics, and Health Economics,* edited by J. van der Gaag and M. Perlman. Amsterdam: North Holland.

Fein, R. 1956. Factors influencing the location of North Carolina general practitioners. Ph.D. dissertation, Johns Hopkins University.

Feldman, J. J. 1966. *The Dissemination of Health Information.* Chicago: Aldine.

Feldstein, P. F. 1983. *Health Care Economics.* New York: Wiley.

Ffrench-Davis, R. 1982. El experimento monetarista en Chile. *Colección Estudios CIEPLAN* 9(December): 5–40.

Foltz, A.; Chen, M.; and Stoga, A. 1977. Public policy and health resource distribution. *Policy Sciences* 8:323–41.

FONASA. 1962–83. Balances Presupuestarios al 31 de Diciembre. Annual financial statements. Mimeo.

―――. 1982.

―――. 1983. Directorio por profesión hasta 17:00 horas del 10-09-83. September 9. Mimeo.

―――. n.d. Frecuencia según cantidad, horario, e item. Mimeo.

―――. n.d. Departmento de Operaciones. Mimeo.

Fotheringham, A. S. 1979. Polarised growth within a multi-growth centre environment: A case study of the United States, 1920–1970. *Environment and Planning A,* 11:193–208.

Foxley, A. 1979. *Redistributive Effects of Government Programmes: The Chilean Case.* Oxford: Pergamon.

Foxley, A., and Raczynski, D. 1984. Vulnerable groups in recessionary situations: The case of children and the young in Chile. *World Development* 12:223–46.

Freidson, E. 1961. *Patients' View of Medical Practice.* New York: Russell Sage.

Friedman, M. 1962. *Capitalism and Freedom.* Chicago: University of Chicago Press.

―――. 1974. Using escalation to fight inflation. *Fortune,* July, 94–97.

Friedman, M., and Friedman, R. 1980. *Free to Choose: A Personal Statement.* New York: Harcourt, Brace, Jovanovich.

Friedmann, J. 1973. *Urbanization, Planning and National Development.* Beverly Hills: Sage.

Fuller, G. 1972. The spatial diffusion of birth control in Chile. PhD. dissertatim, Pennsylvania State University, University Park.

Furst, R. W. 1981. *Financial Management for Health Care Institutions.* Boston: Allyn and Bacon.

Giaconi, J. 1982. Funcionamiento del sistema de servicios de salud. In *Desarrollo Social y Salud en Chile* vol. 3, edited by Hugo Lavados.

Gibson, R. M., ed. 1980 *Health Care Financing Review.* Washington, DC: U.S. Department of Health and Human Services.

Gilbert, A., and Ward, P.M. 1978. Housing in Latin American cities. In *Geography and the Urban Environment,* edited by R. J. Johnston and D. T. Herbert. New York: Wiley.

Goić, A. 1979a. La salud en Chile: El problema de fondo. *Mensaje* 282:558–66.

―――. 1979b. En torno a la medicina social chilena. *Revista Médica de Chile* 107:1043–45.

172 § *Literature Cited*

Griffin E. C., and Ford, L. 1980. A model of Latin American city structure. *Geographical Review* 37:397–422.

Haggett, P. 1976. Hybridizing alternative models of an epidemic diffusion. *Economic Geography* 52:130–40.

Haignere, C. 1982. The application of the free-market economic model in Chile and the effects on its population's health status. School of Public Health, University of Denver, February.

————. 1983. The application of the free-market economic model in Chile and the effects on its population's health status. *International Journal of Health Service.* 13:389–406

Hakim, P., and Solimano, G. 1978. *Development, Reform and Malnutrition in Chile.* Cambridge, MA: MIT Press.

Hall, T. L., and Diaz, S. 1971. Social security and health care patterns in Chile. *International Journal Health Service* 1:363–76.

Hammond, R., and McCullagh, P. S. 1974. *Quantitative Techniques in Geography.* London: Oxford University Press.

Hardoy, J. 1969. Dos mil años de urbanización en América Latina. In *La Urbanización en América Latina,* edited by J. Hardoy and C. Tobar. Buenos Aires: Editorial del Instituto.

Harloe, M. 1981. Notes on comparative urban research. In *Urbanization and Urban Planning in Capitalist Society,* edited by M. Dear and A. J. Scott. New York: Methuen.

Harris, C. 1954. The market as a factor in the localization of industry in the U.S. *Annals of the Association of American Geographers* 44:315–48.

Harris, R. 1984. A political chameleon: Class segregation in Kingston, Ontario, 1961–1975. *Annals of the Association of American Geographers* 74:454–76.

Harvey, D. 1973. *Social Justice and the City.* London: Edward Arnold.

————, 1975. Class structure in a capitalist society and the theory of residential differentiation. In *Progress in Physical and Human Geography,* edited by R. Peet, M. Chisholm, and P. Haggett. London: Heinemann.

Hawley, A. 1950. *Human Ecology: A Theory of Community Structure.* New York: Ronald.

Haynes, K. E., and Fotheringham, A. S. 1984. *Gravity and Spatial Interaction Models.* Beverly Hills: Sage.

Henretta, J. C., and O'Rand, O. M. 1980. Labor force participation of older married women. *Social Security Bulletin* 43:10–16.

Hirschman, A. O. 1970. *Exit, Voice and Loyalty: Responses to Decline in Firms, Organizations, and States.* Cambridge, MA: Harvard University Press.

Hirshleifer, J. 1976. *Price Theory and Applications.* Englewood Cliffs, NJ: Prentice-Hall.

Hodge, D., and Gattrell, A. 1976. Spatial constraint and the location of urban public facilities. *Environment and Planning.* A:215–30.

Homer, C. G. 1982. Some pitfalls in creating competition between HMOs and fee-for-service delivery. *Journal of Health Politics, Policy and Law* 7:687-706.

Hopkins, E. J.; Pye, A. M.; Soloman, M.; and Soloman, S. 1968. The relation of patients' age, sex, and distance from surgery to the demand on the family doctor. *Journal of the Royal College of General Practitioners* 16:368–378.

Hunter, J. M., ed. 1974. *The Geography of Health and Disease.* Studies in Geography no. 6. Chapel Hill: Department of Geography, University of North Carolina.

ILADES (Instituto Latinamoericano de Doctrina y Estudios Sociales). 1984. SPSS computer print out. March.

Illich. I. 1975. *Medical Nemesis: The Expropriation of Health.* London: Calder and Boyars.

INE (Instituto Nacional de Estadísticas). 1979–83. Indices de precios al consumidor.

Ingram, G. K., and Carroll, J. 1981. The spatial structure of Latin American cities. *Journal of Urban Economics* 9:257–72.

Isaac, S., and Michael, W. B. 1981. *Handbook in Research and Evaluation: A Collection of Principles, Methods, and Strategies Useful in the Planning, Design, and Evaluation of Studies in Education and the Behavioral Sciences.* San Diego: Edits Publishers.

Isard, W. 1969. *Methods of Regional Analysis.* New York: Wiley.

James, P. E. 1969. *Latin America.* New York: Odyssey.

Jiménez de la Jara, J. 1982a. Desarrollo y perspectivas del sector privado en salud. In *Desarrollo Social y Salud en Chile* vol. 3, edited by Hugo Lavados, Santiago: CPU.

———. 1982b. Modelo económico y salud. *Vida Médica* December: 37.

Johnston, R. J. 1977. Urban geography: City structures. *Progress in Human Geography.* 1:119–29.

Joseph, A. E. 1981. Measuring potential physical accessibility to general practitioners in urban areas: A methodological note. *New Zealand Geographer* 37:32–34.

Joseph, A. E. 1982. On the interpretation of the coefficient of localization. *Professional Geographer* 34:443–46.

Joseph, A. E., and Bantock, P. R. 1982. Measuring potential physical accessibility to practitioners in rural areas: A method and case study. *Social Science and Medicine* 16:85–90.

Joseph, A. E., and Hall, G. B. 1985. The locational concentration of group homes in Toronto. *Professional Geographer* 37:143–55.

Joseph, A. E., and Phillips, D. 1984. *Accessibility and Utilization: Geographic Perspectives on Health Care Delivery.* London: Harper and Row.

Jud, G. D. 1978. *Inflation and the Use of Indexing in Developing Countries.* New York: Praeger.

Kane, R., and Wilson, W. 1977. The new health practitioner: The past as prologue. *Western Journal of Medicine* 127:254–61.

Kaser, M. 1976. *Health Care in the Soviet Union and Eastern Europe.* Boulder, CO: Westview.

Katz, G.; Mitchell, A.; and Markezin, E. 1982. *Ambulatory Care and Regionalization in Multi-Institutional Health Systems.* Rockville, MD: Aspen.

Kirby, A. 1982. *The Politics of Location.* London: Methuen.

———. 1983. A comment on "Urban structure and geographical access to public services." *Annals of the Association of American Geographers* 73:289–95.

Kirkham, F. T. 1977. Issues in primary care: The 1976 Annual Conference. *Bulletin of the New York Academy of Medicine* 53:7–9.

Knox, P. L. 1978. The intraurban ecology of primary medical care: patterns of accessibility and their policy implications. *Environment and Planning* A:415–35.

———. 1979. The accessibility of primary care to urban patients. *Journal of the Royal College of General Practitioners* 29:160–68.

———. 1980. Measures of accessibility as social indicators. *Social Indicators Research* 7:367–77.

Kohn, R., and White, K. 1976. *Health Care: An International Survey.* New York: Oxford University Press.

Kolakowski, L. 1978. *Main Currents of Marxism,* vols. 1–3. Oxford: Clarendon.

Kornevall, C. 1977. Un cambio en el financiamiento de la seguridad social y sus efectos en el empleo. *El Trimestre Económico* 44:455–82.

Lagos, J. 1984. Departamento de Contabilidad, Central de Abastecimiento. Santiago, June. Unpublished accounting records.

Lawrence, D. 1978. The impact of physician assistants and nurse practitioners on health care access, costs, and quality. *Health and Medical Care Services Review* 1:1–12.

Lee, K., and Mills, A. 1983. *The Economics of Health in Developing Countries.* London: Oxford University Press.

Lefebvre, H. 1978. Reflections on the politics of space. In *Radical Geography,* edited by R. Peet. London: Methuen.

Lineberry, R. 1977. *Equality and Urban Policy.* Beverly Hills: Sage.

Lloyd, P. E., and Dicken, P. 1968. The data bank in regional studies of industry. *Town Planning Review* 38:304–16.

Lomnitz, L. 1978. Mechanisms of articulation between shantytown settlers and the urban center. *Urban Anthropology* 7:185–205.

Longnecker, D. P., 1975. Practice objectives and goals: a survey of family practice and residents. *Journal of Family Practice* 2:342-51.

López, M. A. Expansión de las ciudades. *EURE* 8:31–42.

Luben, J. W.: Reed, I. M.; Worstell, G.; and Drosens, D. 1966. How does distance affect physician activity? *Modern Hospital* 107:8–82.

McCracken, B. H. 1984. Dynamics of growth and change in health care industry. *Economic Review* 59:4–17.

McGee, T. 1971. *The Urbanization Process in the Third World.* London: G. Bell and Sons.

Mach, E. P. 1978. The financing of health systems in developing countries: Discussion paper. *Social Science Medicine* 12 1/C 2/C: 7–11.

McKinlay, J. B., and McKinlay, S. M. 1977. The questionable contribution of medical measures to the decline of mortality in the United States in the twentieth century. *Milbank Memorial Fund Quarterly* 55:405–28.

Malloy, J. M., and Borzutsky, S. 1982. Politics, social welfare policy, and the population problem in Latin America. *International Journal of Health Services* 12:77–91.

Mangin, W. 1967. Latin American squatter settlers: A problem and a solution. *Latin American Research Review* 2:65–98.

Mardones-Santander, F. 1981. Analisis de cinco determinantes del nivel de salud y nutrición infantil: Chile, 1973–79. In *Crecimiento y Desarrollo en la Desnutrición Infantil.* Paris: UNICEF.

Martínez, J., and Tironi, E. 1982. *Materiales para el Estudio de las Clases Medias en la Sociedad Chilena, 1960–1980.* Documento de Trabajo no. 21, December. Documentación Estudios Educación (SUR).

Maxwell, R. 1974. *Health Care, The Growing Dilemma: Need versus Resources in Western Europe, the U.S., and the U.S.S.R.* New York: McKinsey.

May, J. 1950. Medical geography: Its methods and objectives. *Geographical Review* 51:9–41.

———. 1958. *The Ecology of Human Disease.* New York: M. D. Publications.

Mayer, J. 1982. Medical geography: Some unresolved problems. *Professional Geographer* 34:261—69.

Mayhew, L. 1986. *Urban Hospital Location.* London: Allen & Unwin.

Meade, M. 1980. *Conceptual and Methodological Issues in Medical Geography.* Studies in Geography no. 15. Chapel Hill: Department of Geography, University of North Carolina.

Mechanic, D. 1979. Correlates of physician utilization: Why do major multivariate studies of physician utilization find trivial psychosocial and organizational effects? *Journal of Health and Social Behavior* 20:387–96.

Medical World News. 1985. DRGs: How are they stacking up? 11 March.

Medina, E. n.d. Caracteristicas de los problemas de salud y de la atención médica en los diversos subsectores en el Gran Santiago [Characteristics of health and medical problems among different subsystems in Greater Santiago].

Medina, E., and Kaempffer, A. 1982. La salud en Chile durante la década del setenta. *Revista Médica de Chile* 110:1004.

Medina. E., and Yrarrazával, M. 1983. Fiebre tifoidea en Chile: Consideraciones epidemiológicas. *Revista Médica de Chile* 111:609–15.

El Mercurio (Santiago). 1983a. Alzas Superiores al 40% en 30 productos del IPC. 9 October.

———. 1983b. Chile cumplió todas sus metas en salud. 7 November.

———. 1983c. Sistema de salud. 16 November.

———. 1984a. Chile encabeza indices en salud. 3 March.

———. 1984b. Causas de insatisfacción en usarios de salud. 24 March.

———. 1984c. Encuesta de salud. 29 March.

Merrick, T. W. and Schmink, M. 1983. Households headed by women and urban poverty in Brazil. In *Women and Poverty in the Third World*, edited by M. Buvinić, M. A. Lycette and W. P. McGreevey. Baltimore: Johns Hopkins University Press.

Mesa-Lago, C. 1978. *Social Security in Latin America*. Pittsburgh: University of Pittsburgh Press.

Meza, M. E. 1984. ISAPREs: El dilema ante la maternidad. *Paula* 420:60–65.

Ministerio de Salud. 1977. *Políticas de Salud, 1977*. Santiago: Ministerio de Salud.

———. 1982. *Manual para Postas y Consultorios Generales Urbanos y Rurales Traspasados a la Administración Municipal*. Santiago: Ministerio de Salud.

———. 1983. Proyección de morbididad y mortalidad de Chile a mediano plazo. Mimeo.

Mohan, J., and Woods, K. J. 1985. Restructuring health care: The social geography of public and private health care under the British conservative government. *International Journal of Health Services* 15:197–215.

Monroe, C. B., and McGrew, J. C. 1974. Efficiency, equity and multiple facility location. *Proceedings of the Association of American Geographers* 7:142–46.

Morrill, R. L. 1984. The responsibility of geography. *Annals of the Association of American Geographers* 74:1–8.

Morrill, R. L., Earickson, R. J., and Rees, P. 1970. Factors influencing distances travelled to hospitals. *Economic Geography* 46:1–71.

Morrill, R. L., and Kelley, M. 1970. The simulation of hospital use and the estimation of location efficiency. *Geographical Analysis* 2:283–300.

Morris, A. 1981. *Latin America: Economic Development and Regional Differentiation*. New York: Barnes and Noble.

Moscovice, I. 1984. Health care personnel. In *Introduction to Health Services* edited by S. J. Williams and P. R. Torrens. New York: John Wiley.

Municipality of La Florida. 1984. Unpublished socioeconomic data, Department of Social Programs.

Muñoz, H. 1982. *From Dependency to Development*. Boulder, CO: Westview.

Navarro, V. 1974a. What does Chile mean? An analysis of events in the health sector before, during, and after Allende's administration. *Milbank Memorial Fund Quarterly* 52:93–130.

———. 1947b. The underdevelopment of health or the health of underdevelopment. *International Journal of Health Services* 4:5–27.

_____. 1976. *Medicine Under Capitalism.* London: Croom Helm.

Nerlove, M., and Press, S. J. 1973. Univariate and Multivariate Loglinear and Logistic Models. Santa Monica: Rand.

Ochoa, F. 1978. La salud pública en Chile: Analisis de su evolución en el período 1958–1976. Master's thesis, Universidad de Chile.

O'Connor, J. 1973. *The Fiscal Crisis of the State.* New York: St. Martin's.

ODEPLAN (Oficina de Planificación Nacional). 1983. *Informe Social 1982.* Santiago: Presidencia de la República.

O'Donnell, G. 1978. Reflections on the patterns of change in the bureaucratic-authoritarian state. *Latin American Research Review* 13:3–38.

Ostrom, V. 1977. Structure and performance. In *Comparing Urban Service Delivery Systems,* edited by V. Ostrom and F. P. Bish. Beverly Hills: Sage.

PAHO (Pan American Health Organization). 1965. *Health Planning: Problems of Concept and Method.* Science Publication no. 111. Washington, DC: PAHO.

_____. 1982. *Health Conditions in the Americas: 1977–80.* Science Publication no. 427. Washington, DC: PAHO.

Paul, D. W. 1978. Regional physician maldistribution. *Texas Medicine* 74 (May): 114–22.

Peet, J. R. 1975. Inequality and poverty: A Marxist-geographic theory. *Annals of the Association of American Geographers* 65:564–71.

Perlman, J. E. 1976. *The Myth of Marginality, Urban Poverty and Politics in Rio de Janeiro.* Berkeley and Los Angeles: University of California Press.

Petersen, T. 1985. A comment on presenting results from logit and probit models. *American Sociological Review* 50:130–31.

Polgar, S. 1963. Health action in cross-cultural perspective. In *Handbook of Medical Sociology,* edited by E. H. Freeman. Englewood Cliffs, NJ: Prentice-Hall.

Pollarola, F. 1983. Speech at the Colegio Médico, Santiago, 1 July.

Pommerehne, W. W., and Frey, B. S. 1977. Public and private production efficiency in Switzerland: A theoretical and empirical comparison. In *Comparing Urban Service Delivery Systems,* edited by V. Ostrom and F. P. Bish. Beverly Hills: Sage.

Portes, A., and Canak, W. 1981. Latin America: Social structures and sociology. *Annual Reviews* 7:225–48.

Pyle, G. F. 1979. *Applied Medical Geography.* Washington, DC: V. H. Winston.

Quijano, A. 1967. La urbanización de la sociedad en América Latina. *Revista Mexicana de Sociología* 29:669–703.

Raczynski, D. 1982. *Controversias Sobre Reformas al Sector Salud: Chile, 1973–1982.* Notas Técnicas no. 52. Santiago: CIEPLAN.

Raczynski, D., and Oyarzo, D. 1982. ¿Por qué cae la tasa de mortalidad infantil en Chile? *Colección Estudios CIEPLAN* 6:45–84.

Raczynski, D., and Serrano, C. 1984. Mujer y familia en un sector popular urbano: Resultados de un estudio de casos. *Apuntes CIEPLAN* 47.

Rayack, E. 1964. The American Medical Association and the supply of physicians: A study of the internal contradictions in the concept of professionalism. *Medical Care* 2.

Record, J.; McCally, M.; Schweitzer, S.; et al. 1980. New health professions after a decade and a half: Delegation, productivity and costs in primary care. *Journal of Health Politics, Policy and Law* 5:470–97.

Reidy, Angela. 1984. Marxist functionalism in medicine: A critique of the works of Vicente Navarro on health and medicine. *Social Science and Medicine* 19:897–910.

Reilly, B. J. and Fuhr, J. P. 1983. Competition's flawed perspective on the health care market and an alternative approach. *Social Science and Medicine* 17:795–801.

Rezende, F., and Mahar, D. 1981. Saude e previdência social: Uma analise economica, IPEA, Rio de Janeiro, Organización Internacional de Trabajo, Programa de las Naciones Unidas para el Desarrollo (OIT/PNUD). Previsión social del Brazil, Geneva. Mimeo.

Riveros, L. 1983. Distribución del ingreso en el gran Santiago. *Revista de Economía* 9:3–17.

Robert Wood Johnston Foundation. 1978. *America's Health System: A Comparative Analysis*. Special Report no. 1. Princeton, NJ: Robert Wood Johnston Foundation.

Roberts, B. 1978. *Cities of Peasants: The Political Economy of Urbanization in the Third World*. London: Edward Arnold.

Roemer, M. I. 1964. *Medical Care in Latin America*. Washington, DC: Pan American Health Union.

––––––. 1977a. *Comparative National Policies on Health Care*. New York: Marcel Dekker.

––––––. 1977b. *Systems of Health Care*. New York: Springer.

––––––. 1980. Evaluation of health service programs and levels of measurement. In *Issues in Health Services*, edited by S. J. Williams. New York: Wiley.

––––––. 1985. *National Strategies for Health Care Organization: A World Overview*. Ann Arbor, MI: Health Administration Press.

Roemer, M. I., and Schonick, W. 1973. HMO performance: The recent evidence. *Health and Society* 51:271.

Romero, H. 1977. Hitos fundamentales de la medicina social en Chile. In *Medicina Social en Chile*, edited by J. Jiménez de la Jara. Santiago: Aconcagua.

Roos, N. P.; Gaumnot, M.; and Horne, J. M. 1976. The impact of the physician surplus on the distribution of physicians across Canada. *Canadian Public Policy* 2:169–91.

Rosenberg, M. W. 1983a. Accessibility to health care: A North American perspective. *Progress in Human Geography* 7:78–87.

_____. 1983b. Physician location behavior in Metropolitan Toronto. Paper presented at the meeting of the Association of American Geographers, Denver, April.

Rosenthal, S. 1978. Target populations and physicians populations. *Social Science and Medicine* 12 (Medical Geography): 111–15.

Rosenburg, M. 1979. On the location of physicians in metropolitan Toronto, 1951–1971. *Horizon* 37:78–90.

SAS (Statistical Analysis System). 1982. *Statistics.* Carey, NC: SAS.

Saunders, P. 1979. *Urban Politics: A Sociological Interpretation.* London: Hutchinson.

Sayer, A. 1984. *Method in Social Science.* London: Hutchinson.

Scarpaci, J. L. 1983. Utilization of mobile health care services in the Atacama. In *Contemporary Issues in Latin American Geography,* edited by B. Lentneck. Muncie, IN: Conference of Latinamericanist Geographers.

_____. 1984a. Accesibilidad urbana a la atención médica primaria: Estudio comparativo de Canadá, EE.UU. y Chile. *Informaciones Geográficas* 31:33–63.

_____. 1984b. A methodological note on location-allocation models. *American Journal of Public Health* 74:1555–57.

_____. 1985. Restructuring health care financing in Chile. *Social Science and Medicine* 21:415–31.

Scarpaci, J. L.; Infante, P.; and Gaete, A. 1988. Planning Residential Segregation: The Case of Santiago de Chile. *Urban Geography* 9.

Schiel, J., and Wepfer, A. 1976. Distributional aspects of endemic goiter in the United States. *Economic Geography* 52:116–26.

Schmink, M. 1982. *Women in the Urban Economy in Latin America.* Working Paper no. 1. New York: Population Council.

Schneider, H. 1967. Measuring, evaluating and redesigning hospital-physician spatial relationships in metropolitan areas. *Inquiry* 6:24–43.

Schultz, G. P. 1969. *Facility Patterns for a Regional Health Care System.* Discussion Paper no. 34. Philadelphia: Regional Science Research Institute.

Schweitzer, S. O., and Record, J. C. 1977. Third-party payments for new health professionals: An alternative to fractional reimbursement. *Public Health Reports* 92:518–26.

La Segunda (Santiago). 1983. Consultorios de salud. 10 December.

_____. 1984. El gobierno dará un apoyo adicional al presupuesto para mejorar la atención. 8 June.

Servicio de Salud Ambiental. 1983. Bases de un estudio de correlación entre hortalizas, consumos crudos y enfermedades infecciosas. Mimeo.

Shannon, G.; Bashshur, R.; and Spurlock, C. 1978. The search for medical care: An exploration of urban black behavior. *International Journal of Health Services* 8:519–30.

Shannon, G.; Bashshur, R.; and Metzner, C. 1969. The concept of distance as a factor in accessibility and utilization of health care. *Medical Care Review* 26:143–61.

Shannon, G., and Dever, G. E. A. 1974. *Health Care Delivery: Spatial Perspectives.* New York: McGraw-Hill.

Shortell, S. 1980. Factors associated with the utilization of health services. In *Introduction to Health Services,* edited by S. J. Williams and P. R. Torrens. New York: Wiley.

Shouldice, R. G., and Shouldice, K. H. 1978. *Medical Group Practice and Health Maintenance Organizations.* Washington, DC: Information Resources Press.

Sidel, V. 1980. International comparisons of health services: How? Who? Why? *Policy Studies Journal* 9. 300–308.

Sigerist, H. 1947. *Medicine and Health in the Soviet Union.* New York: Citadel.

Sigmund, P. E. 1977. *The Overthrow of Allende and the Politics of Chile.* Pittsburgh: University of Pittsburgh Press.

Silk, J. 1979. *Statistical Concepts in Geography.* London: Allen & Unwin.

Smith, D. 1974. *The Geography of Wellbeing.* New York: McGraw-Hill.

———. 1979. *Human Geography: A Welfare Approach.* London: Edward Arnold.

Solis, F.; Castillo, B.; and Mardones, G. 1982. Mortalidad infantil por causas evitables en los 27 Servicios de Salud del país. *Revista Médica de Chile* 110:383–92.

Sorkin, A. 1976. *Health Economics in Developing Countries.* Lexington, MA: Lexington Books.

Spaulding, W. B., and Spitzer, W. O. 1972. Implications of medical manpower trends in Ontario, 1961–1971. *Ontario Medical Review* 39:527–33.

Spoerel, C. 1974. An analysis of non-hospital based medical practioners' offices in London, Ontario, 1961–1971. Master's thesis, University of Western Ontario.

Spoerer, A. 1973. Doctrina y política de salud, Santiago, Chile. Ministerio de Salud.

Stanislawski, D. 1946. The origin and spread of the grid-pattern town. *Geographical Review* 36:105–20.

———. 1947. Town planning in the New World. *Geographical Review* 37:94–105.

Starr, P. 1982. *The Social Transformation of American Medicine.* New York: Basic Books.

Stockman, D. A., and Gramm, P. W. 1980. The administration's case for hospital cost containment. In *New Directions in Public Health Care,* edited by C. M. Lindsay. San Francisco: Institute for Contemporary Studies.

Stone, D. A. 1980. Obstacles to learning from comparative health research. *Policy Studies Journal* 9:278–85.

Swain, R. W. 1981. *Health Systems Analysis.* Columbus, OH: Grid Publishing.

Symons, R. 1971. Some comments on equity and efficiency in public facility location models. *Antipode* 3:54–67.

Taylor, P. J. 1977. *Distance-Decay in Spatial Interactions.* Catmog 2. Norwich, U.K.: Geo Abstracts.

Tellez, F. P. 1977. Condiciones de salud de la mujer. In *La Mujer y el Desarrollo,* edited by M. L. Leal. Bogata: ACEP.

La Tercera (Santiago). 1983. Entrevista con el Dr. Luis González. 27 March.

Thomas, J., and Hunter, J. 1980. *Internal Migration Systems in the Developing World: With Special Reference to Latin America.* Boston: Hall.

Thrall, G. I., and Tsitandidis, J. 1983. A model of the change attributable to government health insurance plans in location patterns of physicians—with supporting evidence from Ontario, Canada. *Environment and Planning* C:45–55.

Trivelli, P. 1981. Reflexiones en torno a la política nacional de desarrollo urbano. *EURE* 8:43–64.

Tuan, Y-F. 1976. Humanistic geography. *Annals of the Association of American Geographers* 66:266–76.

Turner, J. C. 1968. Housing priorities, settlement patterns and urban development in modernizing countries. *J. of the American Institute of Planners.* 34:354–63.

Ugalde, A. 1978. Health decision making in developing nations: A comparative analysis of Colombia and Iran. *Social Science and Medicine* 12:1–7.

UCFI. 1977. Universidad Católica, Facultad de Ingeniería. Encuesta de origen y destino para el Gran Santiago. Mimeo.

U.S. Embassy (Santiago). 1984. Chile: Economic trends report, September. Mimeo.

Urrutia, G. V. 1975. *Diagnóstico de la Situación de la Mujer Peruana.* Lima: Centro de Estudios de Problación y Desarrollo.

Vekemans, S.; Giusti, J.; and Silva, I. 1970. *Marginalidad, Promoción Popular, e Integración Latinoamericana.* Santiago: DESAL.

Vergara, P. 1981. Las transformaciones de las funciones económicas del estado en Chile bajo el gobierno militar. *Colección Estudios CIEPLAN* 5 (July): 117–54.

Viel, B. 1961. *La Medicina Socializada y su Aplicación en Gran Bretaña, Unión Soviética y Chile.* Santiago: Ediciones de la Universidad de Chile.

de Vise, P. 1971. Cook County Hospital: Bulwark of Chicago's apartheid health system and prototype of nation's public hospitals. *Antipode* 3:9–20.

———. 1973. *Misused and Misplaced Hospitals and Doctors: A Locational Analysis of the Urban Health Care Crisis.* Resource Paper no. 22. Washington, DC: Association of American Geographers.

Viveros-Long, A. M. 1982. Changes in health financing: The Chilean experience. Paper presented at the International Health Conference, Washington, DC, 13–16 June.

Walton, J. 1977. *Elites and Economic Development: Comparative Studies on the Political Economy of Latin American Cities.* Austin: University of Texas Press.

Weil, C., and Kvale, K. M. 1985. Current research on geographical aspects of schistosomiasis. *Geographical Review* 75:186–216.

Wolinsky, F. D., 1978. Assessing the effects of predisposing, enabling, and illness-mobidity characteristics. *Journal of Health and Social Behavior* 19:384–96.

World Bank. 1980. *The World Bank: World Development.* London: Oxford University Press.

Yishai, Y. 1982. Politics and medicine: The case of Israeli national health insurance. *Social Science and Medicine* 16:285–91.

Zalazar, D. 1983a. Algunos hallazgos en antropología de la pobreza en relación a salud. In *III Jornadas Chilenas de Salud Pública: Resumenes de Trabajos Aceptados.* Santiago: Facultad de Medicina, Escuela de Salud Pública, Universidad de Chile.

———. 1983b. Antropología y salud. In *III Jornadas Chilenas de Salud Pública: Resumenes de Trabajos Aceptados.* Santiago: Facultad de Medicina, Escuela de Salud Pública Universidad de Chile.

Zschock, D. K. 1980. Health care financing in Central America and the Andean region. *Latin American Research Review.* 15:169–89.

Zweifel, P. 1982. Fuzzy measurements of output: A problem of evaluation for health policy. *Social Science and Medicine* 16:1291–300.

Index

Accessibility: barriers to, 11; definitions of, 10; deteriorating, most telling sign of, 138; geographic, as component of, 10–11, 140; institutional, 90; models useful in evaluating, 111; in other countries, 11, 90; outcome, as general framework of, 10; primary medical care, components of, 7; in Santiago, 132–35; socioorganizational, as component of, 10–11; structure, as general framework of, 10; surfaces, 112–15, 133; and utilization, 10; to women and those from female-headed households, 90

Administradoras de fondos de pensión (AFPs), 21, 154

Alessandri, Jorge, 32–33

Allende, Salvador: and annual inflation, 57; presidency of (1970–73), 5; "university for all" policy of, 43–44

Ambulatory care. *See* Primary medical care

American Medical Association, 129

Antonovsky's model of utilization and satisfaction, 90

Authoritarian rule. *See* Pinochet, A.

Benefit-cost, studies of, 50

Bismarck, Chancellor, 19

Blue-collar worker. *See Obrero*

Blue Cross and Blue Shield, 56, 58

Bureaucratic-authoritarian state, in Chile, 5

Cajas, 20

Capitation charges, 21, 22

CAT scanners, 60–61

Central de Abastecimiento, 30, 31

Central Place Theory, 129. *See also* Physicians, location of

Centros médicos. See Medical practices, group

Certificate-of-need, 17

Chile: economy of, 41; as modern welfare state, 12. *See also* Alessandri; Allende; Frei; Pinochet

Cities, Latin American, 100–01

Class: and patterns of illness and health, 99; relations, 95; struggle, 92

Coefficient of localization, 123, 126, 141, 165 n.10

Colegio Medico (Chilean Medical Society): defined, 155; and Law Decree 3601, 42; and medical care policy, 42–45; and SERMENA, 25–26

Comité de Acción Social (CAS), 162 n.4. *See also* Villa O'Higgins, neighborhoods of patients at

184 § *Index*

Consultorio periférico. See SNSS, clinics
Consumer price index (CPI), 27, 53, 137–38; in Chile, 1973–76, 13
Consumers: and auxiliary personnel, 138; and costs, 17; and physicians, 16–17; preferences of, 86–88; in siting of clinics, 108

Debt, foreign, 9, 27, 38
Delivery system, 9
Demographic transition, 46
Dental care: demand for, 67; expenditures on, 63
Dentists, wages of, 58–59
Developing nations. *See* Third World
Diagnostic-related groups (DRGs), 56, 129, *et passim*

Economic development, 13, 99, 100
El Nino, and infectious diseases, 49
Empleados, 25

Field irrigation, use of contaminated water for, 50
Fiscal crisis, 53; in Chile, 136
Fiscal retrenchment, 4; in Chilean medical system, 142
FONASA (National Health Fund), 28, 63, 65, 141; availability and accessibility of, 45; breakdown of revenues of, 29; and concentration of general practitioners, 133–34; creation of, 20; and critical care specialists, 118; defined, 155; and levels of care, 115, 137; middle income groups (*empleados*) treated by, 22, 25; and physicians, 115–20; and physician to population ratio, 28; and plastic surgeons, 118; and specialists,

118; supply and demand forces in, 28; and vouchers, 26, 33, 137
Free choice system (*sistema de libre elección*), 26, 57
Frei, Eduardo, health budget of, 32–33

Geographers, 92; Marxist, 97–98; urban, 100
Geography, medical, 7, 94, 96
Gramm, P.W., 15
Gramm-Rudman-Hollings legislation, 4
Gravity model, 111–14
Group practices. *See* Medical practices, group

Health, environmental, 48–51
Health care: definition of, 5; delivery systems, 92; and individual behavior, 4–5
Health care financing, under SNSS, 21
Health care policy: Chilean vs. U.S., 160 *n.8*; evaluation measures of, 45–47; and infant mortality, 46–47; and physician location in Canada and the United States, 127–32
Health Maintenance Organizations (HMOs), 18, 121, 131
Health planning, 133
Health status, 4, 30, 47–48
Help-seeking behavior, 91; and accessibility, 10; and social network, 84; and touching, 163 *n.13*; in Washington, D.C., 131
Hepatitis, 48–50
Herbal remedies, 73, 88
Hill-Burton Act, 129–30
Hospitals, 8, 11

188 § *Index*

PITT LATIN AMERICAN SERIES
Cole Blasier, Editor

Argentina

Argentina in the Twentieth Century
David Rock, Editor

Discreet Partners: Argentina and the USSR Since 1917
Aldo César Vacs

Juan Perón and the Reshaping of Argentina
Frederick C. Turner and José Enrique Miguens, Editors

The Life, Music, and Times of Carlos Gardel
Simon Collier

The Political Economy of Argentina, 1946–1983
Guido DiTella and Rudiger Dornbusch, Editors

Brazil

External Constraints on Economic Policy in Brazil, 1899–1930
Winston Fritsch

The Film Industry in Brazil: Culture and the State
Randal Johnson

The Politics of Social Security in Brazil
James M. Malloy

Urban Politics in Brazil: The Rise of Populism, 1925–1945
Michael L. Conniff

Colombia

Gaitán of Colombia: A Political Biography
Richard E. Sharpless

Roads to Reason: Transportation, Administration, and Rationality in Colombia
Richard E. Hartwig

Cuba

Cuba Between Empires, 1878–1902
Louis A. Pérez, Jr.

Cuba, Castro, and the United States
Philip W. Bonsal

Cuba in the World
Cole Blasier and Carmelo Mesa-Lago, Editors

Cuba Under the Platt Amendment
Louis A. Pérez, Jr.

Cuban Studies, Vols. 16–17
Carmelo Mesa-Lago, Editor

Intervention, Revolution, and Politics in Cuba, 1913–1921
Louis A. Pérez, Jr.

Revolutionary Change in Cuba
Carmelo Mesa-Lago, Editor

*The United States and Cuba: Hegemony and Dependent Development,
1880–1934*
Jules Robert Benjamin

Mexico
The Mexican Republic: The First Decade, 1823–1832
Stanley C. Green

Mexico Through Russian Eyes, 1806–1940
William Harrison Richardson

Oil and Mexican Foreign Policy
George W. Grayson

The Politics of Mexican Oil
Geroge W. Grayson

Voices, Visions, and a New Reality: Mexican Fiction Since 1970
J. Ann Duncan

US Policies
Cuba, Castro, and the United States
Philip W. Bonsal

*The Hovering Giant: U.S. Responses to Revolutionary Change in Latin
America*
Cole Blasier

Illusions of Conflict: Anglo-American Diplomacy Toward Latin America
Joseph Smith

*The United States and Cuba: Hegemony and Dependent Development,
1880–1934*
Jules Robert Benjamin

*The United States and Latin America in the 1980s: Contending
Perspectives on a Decade of Crisis*
Kevin J. Middlebrook and Carlos Rico, Editors